A GUIDE TO
PRONOUNCING
BIBLICAL
NAMES

T.S.K. SCOTT-CRAIG

MOREHOUSE PUBLISHING
A Continuum imprint
HARRISBURG • LONDON • NEW YORK

Morehouse Publishing
P.O. Box 1321
Harrisburg, PA 17105

Morehouse Publishing is a Continuum imprint.

ISBN 0-8192-1292-X

Library of Congress Catalog Card Number 81-84713

Printed in the United States of America

05   06   07   18   17   16

CONTENTS

FOREWORD

This Guide is intended for all who either read the Bible aloud in public or silently to themselves in private.

It provides the currently preferred and permissible pronunciations of some three thousand names (chiefly of people and places) taken from the *New Revised Standard Version* of the Old Testament, the Apocrypha and the New Testament.

The enunciation of names in the Bible is a way of realizing the presence of that WORD which was in the beginning (John 1:1). But conventional spelling is often a poor clue to pronunciation.

For instance, when we see the letters c o u g h, r o u g h, and b o u g h, we are supposed to say "coff," but not "roff" and "boff." When we see the letter "a," we have to choose between the four different sounds in "bat," "dare," "cape" and "calm." Printing the names in phonetic symbols is of little assistance to most of us. They are too difficult to remember. I have therefore devised a simple system of respelling. Only letters of our normal alphabet are used.

A few combinations of these letters will be unfamiliar but will turn out to be helpful. For example:

EH for A as in CAPE or ABEL
OH for O as in OVER or OBED
KH for CH as in BACH or MOLOCH (i.e. when following a vowel)
Y (or EYE) for I as in BITE or JEREMIAH

In the case of names such as Jeremiah or Obadiah, the presence of a "Y" serves to remind us that such names also contain the divine name Yah (i.e., Yahweh).

Each syllable of every word in the respelling is divided from the next by a hyphen. And any syllable to be stressed is followed by a mark of accentuation, commonly called a half slash-mark, (very similar in shape to the acute accent in French). Similar aids to pronunciation have been offered in many Bibles since the middle of the Sixteenth Century, but have confined themselves to what was taken to be the one correct pronunciation. There are, however, in many cases of Biblical names (as indeed in the case of many non-

5

Biblical words) both preferred and permissible pronunciations. In quite a number of instances a permissible pronunciation is therefore placed immediately below what appears to be the preferred one.

It has often been hard to decide between the preferred and the merely permissible—even to decide on what is currently inadmissible. Nevertheless, a two-syllable pronunciation of CANDACE has been ruled out; and likewise the pronunciation of DIVES to rhyme with "hives." Where names like ABRAHAM and CEPHAS have become naturalized in English speech, that usage is given the preference; where that is not so—as in the case of HAROSHETH-HAGOIIM for example—an approximation to the sound in the original tongue has been retained, as at least permissible.

I have tried to keep in mind that we adults were all once children, and that children hear us read aloud. We all learn little words before we learn big words; so it is easy even for adults to say "nap-tha" for "naph-tha" and "nap-tali" for "Naph-tali." Even when we know big words, it is all too easy to give the impression that Azaliah is some kind of azalea. But thanks to radio and television, young and old alike pronounce correctly the last name of the composer BACH; nobody says BAK; so perhaps once again we may hope to hear the same sound in ANTIOCH and MELCHI-ZEDEK.

Names of persons and places have different forms in different books of the Bible. Some are variations of the same name. Others are completely new names for the same person or place. Every variant is listed alphabetically; but, in addition under the main entry, the variants are all listed together, and indicated to be such by being indented one space.

Thus ABRAM (the original form) is followed by an indented ABRAHAM, the later extended form of the same name (and on this occasion, I have, for that reason, not put the two variants in strict alphabetical order).

Thus again, the Old Testament place ACCO (which Israelis again call it) is followed by an indented PTOLEMAIS (which was its name in New Testament times); and then by an indented ACRE (its medieval name, one familiar to many people, but bracketed since it does not actually occur in the text of Scripture). Change of place-names is a well-known phenomenon in our world, not just a Biblical one. When the British left India, the Anglicized place-name BENARES was first restored to BANARAS, and then closer to its original form of VARANASI.

The name HEBER may seem to appear twice, but the English consonants conceal the fact that, in Hebrew, we have here two entirely different names with different connections. But the indentations make clear that the first HEBER is the ancestor of the HEBERITES, while the second HEBER or EBER is the ancestor of the HABIRU, HAPIRU, or HEBREWS.

A short appendix contains Foreign Terms (chiefly Hebrew, Aramaic and Greek) retained in (or implied by) English translations of the Bible; words, names and titles like – "Amen," "Anathema," "Ecclesiastes," "Genesis," "Hallelujah," "Selah" and "Shekinah." Their meaning is therefore given. Most personal names in the Bible, (names like Israel and Jacob, Joshua and Jesus) have also a meaning; these meanings are quite accessible in the appropriate dictionaries and encyclopedias. But one of the personal rewards of my efforts has been to discover that my Christian name "Thomas" (that of the Doubting Apostle) like its Greek equivalent "Didymus," is an Aramaic (originally Phoenician) name, meaning "Twin."

T.S.K. Scott-Craig

Hanover, New Hampshire

AARON	EH'-RON
AARONITE	EH'-RON-IGHT
ABADDON	A-BAD'-ON
ABAGTHA	A-BAG'-THA
ABANA	A-BAH'-NA
ABARIM	A-BAH'-RIMM
ABBA	AB'-BA
ABDA	AB'-DA
ABDEEL	AB'-DE-EL
ABDI	AB'-DE
ABDIEL	AB'-DE-EL
ABDON	AB'-DON
ABEDNEGO	A-BED'-NEG-O
ABEL	EH'-BEL
ABEL-BETH-MAACHAH	EH'-BEL-BETH-MA'-AKH-A
ABELKERAMIM	EH'-BEL-KER-AH'-MIMM
ABELMAIM	EH'-BEL-MAH'-IMM
ABELMEHOLAH	EH'-BEL-MA-HOH'-LA
ABELMIZRAIM	EH'-BEL-MIZ-RAH'-IMM
ABELSHITTIM	EH'-BEL-SHE-TEEM'
ABI	AB'-EYE
ABIALBON	AB'-EE-ALB'-ON
ABIASAPH	AB'-EE-EH'-SAF
EBIASAPH	EB'-EE-EH'-SAF
ABIATHAR	AB-EYE'-A-THAR
ABIB	A'-BIB
ABIDA	AB-EYE'-DA
ABIDAN	AB-EYE'-DAN
ABIEL	AB'-EE-EL
ABIEZER	AB'-EE-EH'-ZER
ABIGAIL	AB'-IGG-EHL
ABIHAIL	AB'-E-HEHL
ABIHU	AB-EYE'-HOO
ABIHUD	AB-EYE'-HOOD
ABIJAH	AB-EYE'-JAH
ABILENE	A'-BILL-EE'-NE
ABIMAEL	AB-IMM'-A-EL
ABIMELECH	AB-IMM'-EL-EKH
ABINADAB	AB-IN'-A-DAB
ABINOAM	AB-IN-OH'-AM
ABIRAM	AB-EYE'-RAM
ABISHAG	AB-EYE'-SHAG

ABISHAI	AB-EYE'-SHY
ABISHALOM	AB-ISH'-A-LOMM
ABISHUA	AB-ISH'-OO-A
ABISHUR	AB-EYE'-SHURR
ABITAL	AB-EYE'-TAL
ABITUB	AB-EYE'-TOOB
ABIUD	AB-EYE'-OOD
ABNER	AB'-NER
ABRAM	EHB'-RAM
	AB'-RAM
ABRAHAM	EHB'-RA-HAM
	AB'-RA-HAM
ABRON	A'-BRON
ABRONAH	A-BROH'-NA
ABSALOM	AB'-SAL-OMM
ABUBUS	A-BOO'-BUS
ACCAD	AK'-ADD
ACCO	AK'-O
	AK'-KO
PTOLEMAIS	TOL-E-MEH'-ISS
[ACRE]	[EHK'-ER]
ACCOS	AK'-OSS
ACHAIA	A-KY'-A
ACHAICUS	A-KY'-A-CUSS
ACHAN	AKH'-AN
ACHBOR	AKH'-BOR
ACHIM	AH'-KIMM
ACHIOR	AH'-KEY-OR
ACHISH	AKH'-ISH
ACHOR	AKH'-OR
ACHSAH	AKH'-SA
ACHSHAPH	AKH'-SHAFF
ADAR	AH'-DAR
ADASA	A-DAS'-A
ADBEEL	AD'-BEE-EL
ADDAN	ADD'-AN
ADDON	ADD'-ON
ADDAR	ADD'-AR
ADDI	ADD'-EE
ADIDA	A'-DID-A
ADIEL	A'-DEE-EL
ADIN	AH'-DEEN
ADINA	A'-DIN-A

ADITHAIM	A'-DITH-AH'-IMM
ADLAI	ADD'-LAY
ADMAH	ADD'-MA
ADMATHA	ADD-MA'-THA
ADMIN	ADD'-MINN
ADNA	ADD'-NA
ADONIBEZEK	ADD'-ON-EE-BEZ'-EK
ADONIJAH	ADD-ON-EYE-'JAH
ADONIKAM	ADD-ON-EYE-'KAM
ADONIRAM	ADD-ON-EYE-'RAM
ADONIZEDEK	ADD-ON-EE-ZED'-EK
ADORAIM	ADD'-OR-AH'-IMM
ADORAM	ADD-OH'-RAM
ADRAMMELECH	A-DRAM'-EL-EKH
ADRAMYTTIUM	A'-DRA-MIT'-EE-OOM
ADRIA	AH'-DREE-A
ADRIEL	AH'-DREE-EL
ADUEL	A-DOO'-EL
ADULLAM	A-DULL'-AM
ADUMMIM	A-DOOM'-IMM
AENEAS	A-NEE'-US
AENON	EH'-NONN
AESORA	EH-SORE'-A
AGABUS	AG'-A-BUS
AGAG	EH'-GAG
AGAGITE	EH'-GAG-IGHT
AGEE	AH'-GEH
AGIA	AH'-GEH-A
AGRIPPA	A-GRIP'-A
AGUR	AH'-GOOR
AHAB	EH'-HAB
AHARAH	A-HA'-RA
AHARHEL	A-HAR'-HELL
AHASBAI	A-HAS'-BY
AHASUERUS	A-HAS'-YOU-EHR'-US
AHAVA	A-HAH'-VA
AHAZ	EH'-HAZ
AHAZIAH	A-HAZ-EYE'-A
AHBAN	AH'-BAN
AHER	AH'-HER
AHI	AH'-HE
AHIAH	A-HIGH'-A
AHIAM	A-HIGH'-AM

11

AHIAN	A-HIGH'-AN
AHIEZER	A-HE-EH'-ZER
AHIHUD	A-HIGH'-OOD
AHIJAH	A-HIGH'-JA
AHIKAM	A-HIGH'-KAM
AHIKAR	A-HIGH'-KAR
AHILUD	A-HIGH'-LOOD
AHIMAAZ	A-HIM'-A-AS
AHIMAN	A-HIM'-AN
AHIMELECH	A-HIM'-EL-EKH
AHIMOTH	A-HIGH'-MOHTH
AHINADAB	A-HIN'-A'-DAB
AHINOAM	A-HIN-OH'-AM
AHIO	A-HIGH'-OH
AHIRA	A-HIGH'-RA
AHIRAM	A-HIGH'-RAM
AHISAMACH	A-HIS'-A-MAKH
AHISHAHAR	A-HISH'-A-AR
AHISHAR	A-HIGH'-SHAR
AHITHOPHEL	A-HITH'-O-FEL
AHITUB	A-HIGH'-TOOB
AHLAB	A'-LAB
AHLAI	A'-LIE
AHOAH	A-HO'-A
AHOHI	A-HO'-HE
AHOHITE	A-HO'-HIGHT
AHOLIBAMAH	A-HOLLY-BA'-MA
AHUMAI	A-HOO'-MY
AHUZZAM	A-HUZZ'-AM
AHUZZATH	A-HUZZ'-ATH
AHZAI	AZ'-EYE
AI	EH'-EYE
	AH'-EYE
AIAH	EYE'-YA
AIATH	EYE'-YATH
AIJA	EYE'-YA
AIJALON	EYE'-YA-LON
	ADJ'-A-LON
AIN	EHN'
AKAN	EH'-CAN
AKELDAMA	A-KEL'-DA-MA
AKKUB	AK'-UBB
AKRABATTENE	AK'-RA-BAT'-A-NAY

AKRABBIM	AK-RABB'-IMM
ALCIMUS	AL'-SIM-US
ALEMA	AL'-E-MA
ALEMETH	AL'-EM-ETH
ALEXANDER	AL'-EX-AND'-ER
	AL'-IG-ZAND'-ER
ALEXANDRA	AL'-EX-AN'-DRA
	AL'-IG-ZAN'-DRA
ALEXANDRIA	AL'-EX-AN'-DRE-A
	AL'-IG-ZAN'-DRE-A
ALIAH	AL'-EE-A
ALIAN	AL'-EE-AN
ALLAMMELECH	A-LAM'-A-LEK
ALLON	AL'-ON
ALLON-BACUTH	AL'-ON-BAK'-UTH
ALMODAD	AL-MOH'-DAD
ALMON	AL'-MON
ALMON-DIBLATHAIM	AL'-MON-DIB'-LA-THA'-IMM
ALPHAEUS	AL-FEE'-US
ALUSH	AH'-LUSH
ALVAH	AL'-VAH
ALVAN	AL'-VAN
AMAD	AH'-MAD
AMALEK	AM'-AL-EK
AMALEKITES	AM-AL'-EK-IGHTS
AMAM	AH'-MAM
AMANA	A-MAH'-NA
AMARIAH	AM-A-RYE'-A
AMASA	A-MAH'-SA
AMASHI	A-MAH'-SIGH
AMASHAI	A-MASH'-EYE
AMASIAH	AM'-A-SIGH'-A
AMAW	AH'-MAW
AMAZIAH	AM'-A-ZY'-A
AMI	AH'-MY
AMITTAI	A-MITT'-EYE
AMMAH	AM'-AH
AMMI	AM'-EYE
AMMIDIANS	A-MID'-E-ANS
AMMIEL	AM'-E-EL
AMMIHUD	A-MY'-HOOD
AMMINADAB	A-MINN'-A-DAB
AMMISHADDAI	A'-MISH-ADD'-EYE

AMMIZABAD	A-MIZ'-A-BAD
AMMON	AM'-ON
AMMONITES	AM'-ON-IGHTS
AMNON	AM'-NON
AMOK	AH'-MAWK
AMON	AM'-ON
AMORITES	AM'-OR-IGHTS
AMOS	EH'-MOSS
AMOZ	AH'-MOZ
AMPHIPOLIS	AM-FIP'-OLL-ISS
AMPLIATUS	AM'-PLEA-AH'-TUSS
AMRAM	AM'-RAM
AMRAMITES	AM'-RAM-IGHTS
AMRAPHEL	AM'-RA-FELL
HAMMURABI	HAM'-URR-AB'-BE
AMZI	AM'-ZY
ANAB	AH'-NAB
ANAEL	AN'-E-EL
ANAH	AH'-NA
ANAHARATH	A-NAH'-A-RATH
ANAIAH	AN-EYE'-A
	A-NAH'-YA
ANAK	AH'-NAK
ANAMIM	AN'-A-MIMM
ANAMMELECH	A-NAM'-A-LEK
ANAN	AH'-NAN
ANANI	A-NAH'-NEE
ANANIAH	AN-A-NIGH'-A
ANANIAS	AN-A-NIGH'-ASS
ANANIEL	A-NAN'-E-EL
ANASIB	AN'-A-SIB
ANATH	AH'-NATH
ANATHOTH	AN'-A-THOTH
ANATHOTHITE	AN'-A-THO-THIGHT
ANDREW	AN'-DREW
ANDRONICUS	AN-DRON'-E-CUSS
ANEM	AH'-NEM
ANER	AH'-NER
ANIAM	A-NIGH'-AM
ANIM	AH'-NIM
ANNA	ANN'-A
ANNAN	ANN'-AN
ANNAS	ANN'-ASS

14

ANNIAS	A-NIGH'-ASS
ANNIUTH	A-NIGH'-ETH
ANNUNUS	A-NOON'-US
ANTHOTHIJAH	AN'-THOH-THIGH'-YA
ANTIOCH	AN'-TEE-OK
	AN'-TEE-OCH
ANTIOCHIANS	AN'-TEE-OK'-IANS
ANTIOCHIS	AN-TIGH'-O-KISS
	AN-TIGH'-OCH-ISS
ANTIOCHUS	AN-TIGH'-OK-USS
	AN-TIGH'-OCH-USS
ANTIPAS	AN'-TIP-ASS
ANTIPATER	AN-TIP'-ATER
ANTIPATRIS	AN-TIP'-A-TRISS
ANUB	AH'-NOOB
APAME	A-PAH'-ME
APELLES	A-PEL'-IS
APHAIREMA	A-FIGH-REH'-MA
APHEK	AH'-FEK
APHERRA	A-FER'-A
APHIAH	A-FEE'-A
	A-FIGH'-A
APHIK	AH'-FIK
APIS	AH'-PISS
APOLLONIA	A-POLL-OH'-NE-A
APOLLONIUS	A-POLL-OH'-NE-US
APOLLOPHANES	A-POLL-OFF'-A-NAYS
APOLLOS	A-POLL'-OSS
APPAIM	AP'-E-IMM
APPHIA	A'-FEE-A
APPIUS	A'-PEE-US
AQUILA	AK'-WILL-A
AR	AER'
ARA	AR'-A
ARAB	AR'-AB
ARABAH	AR'-A-BA
ARABIA	A-REH'-BI-A
ARABIANS	A-REH'-BE-ANS
ARAD	AH'-RADD
ARADUS	AR'-A-DUSS
ARAH	AH'-RA
ARAM	AR'-AM
ARAMEANS	AR-A-ME'-ANS

ARAMITESS	AR-AM-IT'-ESS
ARAM-MAACAH	AR'-AM-MAH'-A-KA
ARAM-NAHARAIM	AR'-AM-NAH'-A-RAH'-EEM
ARAM-ZOBAH	AR'-AM-ZOH'-BA
ARAN	AR'-AN
ARARAT	AR'-A-RAT
ARAUNAH	A-RAW'-NA
ARBA	AR'-BA
ARBATHITE	AR'-BA-THIGHT
ARBATTA	AR-BAT'-A
ARBELA	AR-BEHL'-A
ARBITE	AR'-BIGHT
ARCHELAUS	AR-KA-LEH'-US
	AR-CHA-LEH'-US
ARCHIPPUS	AR-KIP'-US
	AR-CHIPP-US
ARCHITE	AR'-KIGHT
ARD	ARD'
ARDAT	AR'-DAT
ARDITES	AR'-DIGHTS
ARDON	AR'-DON
ARELI	A'-REH-LIE
ARELITES	A'-REL-IGHTS
AREOPAGITE	AR-E-OP'-A-GIGHT
	AR-E-OP'-A-JIGHT
AREOPAGUS	AR-E-OP'-A-GUSS
ARETAS	AR'-E-TASS
ARGOB	AR'-GOBB
ARIARTHES	AR-I-ARTH'-EHS
ARIDAI	AR-ID-EYE'
ARIDATHA	AR-A-DAH'-THA
ARIEH	AR'-E-EH
ARIEL	AR'E-EL
ARIMATHEA	AR'-E-MATH-EH'-A
ARIOCH	AR'-E-OKK
ARISAI	AR'-E-SIGH
ARISTARCHUS	AR-ISS-TAR'-KUSS
	AR-ISS-TAR'-CHUSS
ARISTEAS	AR-ISS-TEH'-AS
ARISTOBULUS	AR-ISS-TOBB'-YEW-LUSS
	AR-ISS'-TO-BOOL-USS
ARIUS	AR'-E-USS
ARKITE	AR'-KIGHT
ARMAGEDDON	AR-MA-GEDD'-ON

ARMONI	AR-MOH'-NEE
ARNA	AR'-NA
ARNAN	AR'-NAN
ARNI	AR'-NIGH
ARNON	AR'-NON
AROD	AR'-ODD
ARODI	AR'-O-DEE
ARODITES	AR'-O-DIGHTS
AROER	AR-ROH'-ER
AROERITE	A-ROH'-ER-IGHT
AROM	AR'-OMM
ARPACHSHAD	AR-PAK'-SHAD
ARPAD	AR'-PAD
ARSACES	AR'-SA-SEZ
ARTAXERXES	AR-TAX-ERK'-SEES
ARTEMAS	AR'-TEM-ASS
ARTEMIS	AR'-TEM-ISS
DIANA	DYE-AN'-A
ARUBBOTH	A-RUB'-OTH
ARUMAH	A-ROO'-MA
ARVAD	AR'-VAD
ARVADITE	AR'-VA-DIGHT
ARZA	ARTS'-A
ARZARETH	ARTS'-A-RETH
ASA	EH'-SA
ASAHEL	AS'-A-HELL
ASAIAH	AS-EYE'-A
ASAPH	EH'-SAFF
ASARAMEL	A-SAR'-A-MEL
ASAREL	AS'-A-REL
ASENATH	AS'-AN-ATH
ASHAN	AH'-SHAN
ASHARELAH	ASH-A-REH'-LA
ASHBEL	ASH'-BELL
ASHBELITES	ASH'-BEL-IGHTS
ASHDOD	ASH'-DODD
ASHER	ASH'-ER
ASHERITE	ASH'-ER-IGHT
ASHERAH	ASH'-ERR-A
ASHERIM	ASH'-ERR-EEM
ASHEROTH	ASH-ERR-OATH
ASHHUR	ASH'-ER
ASHIMA	ASH'-IMM-A

ASHIMAH	ASH'-IMM-A
ASHKELON	ASH'-KA-LON
ASKALON	ASK'-A-LON
ASHKENAZ	ASH'-KE-NAZ
ASHPENAZ	ASH'-PE-NAZ
ASHTAROTH	ASH'-TAR-OTH
	ASH'-TAR-OATH
ASHTERATHITE	ASH'-TER-A-THIGHT
ASHTEROTH-KARNAIM	ASH'-TER-OTH-KAR-NAH'-IMM
	ASH'-TER-OATH-KAR-NAH'-EEM
ASHTORETH	ASH'-TOH-RETH
ASHURBANIPAL	ASH'-URR-BA'-NIP-AL
	ASS'-URR-BA'-NIP-AL
ASHURITES	ASH'-ER-IGHTS
ASHVATH	ASH'-VATH
ASIA	EH'-ZHA
	EH'-SHA
ASIARCH	EH'-ZHE-ARK
	EH'-ZHE-ARCH
ASIDEANS	A-SID'-E-ANS
ASIEL	AS'-E-EL
ASMODEUS	AZ-MODE'-E-USS
	AZ-MO-DEH'-USS
ASNAH	AS'-NA
ASPATHA	AS-PA'-THA
ASPHAR	AS'-FAR
ASRIEL	AS'-RE-EL
ASSHUR	ASH'-URR
	ASS'-URR
ASSHURIM	ASH'-ER-IMM
ASSIDIANS	ASS-IDD'-E-ANS
ASSIR	ASS'-EER
ASSOS	ASS'-OSS
ASSYRIA	ASS-IRR'-I-A
ASTYAGES	AS-TIGH'-A-GEHS
ASUR	A'-SOOR
ASYNCRITUS	A-SINK'-RI-TUSS
ATAD	AH'-TADD
ATARAH	AT'-A-RA
ATARGATIS	AT-AR-GA'-TISS
ATAROTH	AT'-AR-OTH
ATAROTH-ADDAR	AT'-AR-OTH-ADD'-AR
ATBASH	AT'-BASH
ATER	EH'-TER

ATHACH	EH'-THAK
ATHAIAH	A-THEH-EYE'-A
ATHALIAH	A-THAL-EYE'A
ATHARIAS	ATH-AR-EYE'ASS
ATHARIM	ATH'-AR-IMM
ATHENOBIUS	ATH-ENN-OH'-BE-USS
ATHENS	ATH'-ENNS
ATHLAI	ATH'-LIGH
ATROTH-BETH-JOAB	AT'-ROTH-BETH-JOE'-AB
ATROTH-SHOPHAN	AT'-ROTH-SHOH'-FAN
ATTAI	AT'-EYE
ATTALIA	AT'-AL-EYE'-A
ATTALUS	AT'-AL-USS
ATTHARATES	ATH'-A-RAH'-TEHS
ATTHARIAS	ATH'-AR-EYE'-ASS
AUGUSTUS	A-GUSS'-TUSS
	AW-GUSS'-TUSS
AURANUS	AW-RA'-NUSS
	A-REH'-NUSS
AVARAN	AV'-A-RAN
AVEN	AH'-VENN
AVVA	A'-VA
AVVIM	AV'-IMM
AVVITES	A'-VIGHTS
AYYAH	AH'-YA
AZAEL	AZ'-E-EL
AZALIAH	AZ'-A-LIE'-A
AZANIAN	AZ'-A-NIGH'-A
AZAREL	AZ'-A-REL
AZARIAH	AZ-AR-EYE'-A
AZARIAS	AZ-AR-EYE'-AS
AZARU	AZ'-A-ROO
AZAZ	AH'-ZAZ
AZAZIAH	AZ-AZ-EYE'-A
AZBUK	AZ'-BUCK
AZEKAH	A-ZEH'-KA
AZEL	A'-ZELL
AZETAS	A-ZEH'-TASS
AZGAD	AZ'-GAD
AZIEL	A'-ZE-EL
AZIZA	AZ-EYE'-ZA
AZMAVETH	AZ'-MA-VETH
AZMON	AZ'-MON

19

AZNOTH-TABOR	AZ'-NOTH-TEH'-BORR
AZOR	A'-ZOR
AZOTUS	AZ-OH'-TUSS
AZRIEL	AZ'-RI-EL
AZRIKAM	AZ'-RI-KIMM
AZUBAH	A-ZOO'-BA
AZZAN	AZ'-AN
AZZUR	AZ'-ER

– B –

BAAL	BA'-AL
	BEHL'
BAALAH	BA'-A-LA
BAALATH	BA'-A-LATH
BALLATH-BEER	BA'-A-LATH-BEH'-ER
BAAL-BERITH	BA'-AL-BIR-EETH
BAALE-JUDAH	BA'-AL-E-JOO-DA
BAAL-GAD	BA'-AL-GAD
BAAL-HAMON	BA'-AL-HA'-MON
BAAL-HANAN	BA'-AL-HA'-NAN
BAAL-HAZOR	BA'-AL-HA'-ZOR
BAAL-HERMON	BA'-AL-HER'-MON
BAALI	BA'-AL-EYE
BAALIM	BA'-AL-IMM
BAALIS	BA'-AL-ISS
BAAL-MEON	BA'-AL-MEH'-ON
BAAL-PEOR	BA'-AL-PEH'-OR
BAAL-PERAZIM	BA'-AL-PE-RAZ'-IMM
BAALSAMUS	BA'-AL-SA'-MUSS
BAAL-SHALISHAH	BA'-AL-SHAL'-E-SHA
BAAL-TAMAR	BA'-AL-TA'-MAR
BAALZEBUB	BA'-AL-ZE-BUBB'
BAAL-ZEPHON	BA'-AL-ZE-FON'
BAANA	BA'-A-NA
BAANAH	BA'-A-NA
BAARA	BA'-A-RA
BAASEIAH	BA'-AS-EYE'-A
BASSHA	BA'-A-SHA
BABEL	BEH'-BEL
BABYLON	BAB'-EL-ON
BACA	BA'-KA
BACCHIDES	BAK'-A-DAYS
BACENOR	BA-KEH'-NOR
	BA-SAY'-NOR

BAEAN	BEH'-AN
BAGOAS	BA-GO'-ASS
BAHARUM	BA-HAR'-EM
BAHURIM	BA'-HOO'-RIM
BAITERUS	BA'-TER-USS
	BY'-TER-USS
BAKBAKKAR	BAK-BAK'-ER
BAKBUKIAH	BAK-BA-KIGH'-A
BALAAM	BEH'-LAMM
BALADAN	BAL'-A-DAN
BALAH	BAH'-LA
BALAK	BEH'-LAK
BALAMON	BAL'-A-MON
BALBAIM	BAL-BEH'-IMM
BAMOTH	BEH'-MOTH
	BEH'-MOATH
BAMOTH-BAAL	BEH'-MOATH-BA'-AL
BANI	BEH'-NIGH
BANNAS	BAN'-ASS
BARABBAS	BA-RABB'-ASS
BARACHEL	BAR'-AKH-EL
BARACHIAH	BAR-A-KI'-A
	BAR-A-CHI'-A
BARAK	BEH'-RAK
	BA'-RAK
BARIAH	BAR-EYE'-A
BAR-JESUS	BAR-JEE'-ZUSS
BAR-JONA	BAR-JOE'-NA
BARKOS	BAR'-KOSS
BARNABAS	BAR'-NA-BASS
BARODIS	BA-ROH'-DISS
BARSABBAS	BAR-SABB'-ASS
	BAR'-SA-BASS
BARTACUS	BAR'-TA-CUSS
BARTHOLOMEW	BAR-THOLL'-O-MEW
BARTIMAEUS	BAR-TI-MEH'-USS
BARUCH	BAR'-OOK
	BAR'-UGH
BARZILLAI	BAR-ZIL'-EYE
BASEMATH	BA'-SE-MATH
BASHAN	BEH'-SHAN
	BA'-SHAN
BASKAMA	BASS'-KA-MA
BATH-RABBIM	BATH-RABB'-IM

BATH-SHUA	BATH-SHOO'-A
BAWI	BAV'-EYE
BAZLITH	BAZ'-LITH
BAZLUTH	BAZ'-LOOTH
BEALIAH	BA-AL-EYE'-A
BEALOTH	BA'-AL-OTH
BEBAI	BEH'-BY
BECORATH	BE-KORR'-ATH
BECTILETH	BEEK'-TILL-ETH
BEDAD	BID-ADD'
BEDAN	BID-ANN'
BEDEIAH	BID-EYE'-A
BEELIADA	BE-EL-EYE'-A-DA
[BAALIADA]	[BA-AL-EYE'-A-DA]
ELIADA	EHL-I-A'-DA
BEELZEBUL	BE-EL'-ZEE-BULL
BEER	BA-EEHR'
BEERA	BA-EH'-RA
BEERAH	BA-EH'-RA
BEER-ELIM	BA-ER-EH'-LEEM
BEERI	BA-EH'-REE
BEER-LAHAI-ROI	BA-ER-LA'-HIGH-ROH'-EE
BEEROTH	BA-EH'-ROTH
BEEROTHITE	BA-EH'-RA-THIGHT
BEEROTH BENE-JAAKAN	BA-EH'-ROTH-BA-NEH'-YAH'-A-KA
BEER-SHEBA	BA-EHR'-SHEEB-A'
	BEER-SHE'-BA
BE-ESHTERAH	BA-ESH'-TER-A
BEHEMOTH	BA-HEH'-MOATH
	BE'-HIM-OTH
BEL	BELL'
BELA	BEH'-LA
BELIAL	BEE'-LE-AL
BELMAIN	BEL'-MEHN
BALAMON	BAL'-A-MON
BALBAIM	BAL'-BEHM
BELNUUS	BEL'-NOO-US
BELSHAZZAR	BEL-SHADS'-AR
BELTESHAZZAR	BEL-TE-SHADS'-AR
BELTETHMUS	BAL-TETH'-MUSS
BEN-ABINADAB	BEN-A-BIN'-A-DAB
BENAIAH	BE-NAH'-YA
	BEN-EYE'-A

BEN-AMMI	BEN-AM'-EYE
BEN-DEKER	BEN-DEE'-KERR
BENE-BERAK	BEN-IH-BIRR'-AK
BENE-JAAKAN	BEN-IH'-JAH'-A-CAN
BEN-GEBER	BEN-GEB'-BER
BEN-HADAD	BEN-HAY'-DAD
	BEN-HAD'-AD
BEN-HAIL	BEN-HA'-ILL
BEN-HANAN	BEN-HA'-NAN
BEN-HESED	BEN-HESS'-EDH
BEN-HINNOM	BEN-HIN'-OHM
BEN-HUR	BEN-HER'
BENINU	BEN-EYE'-NOO
BENJAMIN	BEN'-JAM-INN
BENJAMITE	BEN'-JA-MIGHT
BENO	BE-NOH'
	BE'-NOH
BEN-ONI	BEN-OH'-NEE
BEN-ZOHETH	BEN-ZOH'-HETH
BEON	BE-OHN'
	BE'-ON
BEOR	BE-OHR'
	BE'-OR
BERA	BE-RA'
	BE'-RA
BERACHAH	BER-AKH'-AH
BERAIAH	BER-EYE'-AH
BEREA	BER-EE'-AH
BERECHIAH	BER-EKH-EYE'-AH
BERED	BE-REDH'
BERI	BEH'-REE
BERIAH	BE-RYE'-AH
BERIITES	BE-RYE'-IGHTS
BERNICE	BER-NEESS'
BEROEA	BE-REE'-A
BEROTHAH	BER-OATH'-A
BEROTHAI	BER-OATH'-EYE
BESAI	BEH'-SIGH
BESCASPASMYS	BESS'-KASS-PAZ'-MOSS
BESODEIAH	BESS-OADH-EYE'-AH
BESOR	BE-ZOHR'
BETAH	BET'-AH
BETEN	BET'-ENN

BETHABARA	BETH-AB'-AR-A
BETH-ANATH	BETH-AH'-NATH
BETH-ANOTH	BETH-AH'-NOTH
BETHANY	BETH'-A-NEE
BETH-ARABAH	BETH-AR-AH'-BA
BETH-ARBEL	BETH-AR'-BELL
BETH-ASHBEA	BETH-ASH-BE-A
BETH-ASMOTH	BETH-AS'-MOTH
BETH-AVEN	BETH-EH'-VEN
BETH-AZMAVETH	BETH-AZ'-MA-VETH
BETH-BAAL-MEON	BETH-BA'-AL-MEH'-ON
BETH-BARAH	BETH-BAH'-RA
BETHBASI	BETH-BAZ'-E
BETH-BIRI	BETH-BIR'-E
BETH-CAR	BETH-KAR'
BETH-DAGON	BETH-DAH'-GON
	BETH-DEH'-GON
BETH-DIBLATHAIM	BETH'-DIBB-LA-THAH'-IM
BETH-EDEN	BETH-EH'-DEN
BETH-EGLAIM	BETH-EGG'-LE-IM
BETH-EKED	BETH-EH'-KEDD
BETHEL	BETH'-EL
	BETH-EHL'
BETH-EMEK	BETH-EH'-MEK
BETHER	BETH'-ER
BETHESDA	BETH-EZ'-DA
BETH-EZEL	BETH-EH'-ZEL
BETH-GADER	BETH-GAH'-DER
BETH-GAMUL	BETH-GAH'-MOOL
BETH-GILGAL	BETH-GILL'-GAL
BETH-HACCHEREM	BETH-HAK'-ER-EM
BETH-HAGGAN	BETH-HAG'-AN
BETH-HARAM	BETH-HAH'-RAM
BETH-HARAN	BETH-HAH'-RAN
BETH-HOGLAH	BETH-HOG'-LA
BETH-HORON	BETH-HOH'-RONN
BETH-JESHIMOTH	BETH-JESH'-IMM-OTH
BETH-LE-APHRAH	BETH-LE-AFF'-RA
BETH-LEBAOTH	BETH-LE-BAH'-OTH
BETHLEHEM	BETH'-LE-HEM
	BETH-LEKH'-EM
BETHLEHEMITE	BETH'-LE-HEM-IGHT
BETH-MAACAH	BETH-MAH'-A-KA

24

BETH-MARCABOTH	BETH-MAHR'-KA-BOTH
BETH-MEON	BETH-MEH'-ON
BETH-MILLO	BETH-MILL'-O
BETH-NIMRAH	BETH-NIMM-RA
BETH-PAZZEZ	BETH-PAZ'-IZ
BETH-PELET	BETH-PEH'-LIT
BETH-PEOR	BETH-PEH'-OR
BETHPHAGE	BETH'-FA-GEH
BETH-RAPHA	BETH-RAH'-FA
BETH-REHOB	BETH-REH'-HOB
BETH-SAIDA	BETH-SEH'-E-DA
BETH-SHAN	BETH-SHAN'
BETHSHAN	BETH-SHAN'
BETH-SHEAN	BETH-SHEH'-AN
SCYTHOPOLIS	SCITH-OPP'-O-LISS
BETH-SHEMESH	BETH-SHEM'-ISH
BETH-SHITTAH	BETH-SHE'-TA
BETH-TAPPUAH	BETH-TAP'-YOO-A
BETHUEL	BETH-OU'-EL
BETHULIA	BETH-OU'-LI-A
BETH-ZAITH	BETH-ZAH'-ITH
BETH-ZATHA	BETH-ZAH'-THA
BETH-ZECHARIAH	BETH-ZEK'-AR-EYE'-A
BETH-ZUR	BETH-ZOOR'
BETOMASTHAIM	BET'-O-MESS-THAH'-EM
BETONIM	BE-TOHN'-IM
BEULAH	BEW'-LA
BEZAI	BEHZ'-EYE
BEZALEL	BEZ'-A-LELL
BEZEK	BEH'-ZEK
BEZER	BEH'-ZER
BICHRI	BIKH'-RYE
BICHRITES	BIKH'-RIGHTS
BIDKAR	BID'-KAR
BIGTHA	BIG'-THA
BIGTHAN	BIG'-THAN
BIGTHANA	BIG-THA'-NA
BIGVAI	BIGV'-EYE
BILDAD	BILL'-DAD
BILEAM	BILL'-E-AM
BILGAH	BILL'-GAH
BILGAI	BILL'-GEYE
BILHAH	BILL'-HA

BILHAN	BILL'-HAN
BILSHAN	BILL'-SHAN
BIMHAL	BIMM'-HAL
BINEA	BINN'-E-A
BINNUI	BINN'-YOO-EYE
BELNUUS	BEL'-NOO-US
BIRSHA	BIRSH'-A
BIRZAITH	BIR-ZAH'-ITH
BISHLAM	BISH'-LEM
BITHIAH	BITH-EYE'-A
BITHYNIA	BITH-INN'-I-A
BIZIOTHIAH	BIZZ'-I-OH-THIGH'-A
BIZTHA	BIZZ'-THA
BLASTUS	BLAST'-OS
BOANERGES	BOH'-AN-ER'-JEZ
BOAZ	BOH'-AZ
BOCHERU	BOH'KHER-OO
BOCHIM	BOH'-KHIMM
BOHAN	BOH'-HAN
BORASHAN	BOH-RAH'-SHAN
BORITH	BOH'-RITH
BOSOR	BOH'-SOR
BOUGAEAN	BOO-GEH'-AN
BOZEZ	BOH'-ZIZZ
BOZKATH	BOHZ'-KATH
BOZRAH	BOZZ'-RA
BUKKI	BUKK'-EYE
BUKKIAH	BUKK-EYE'-A
BUL	BOOL'
BUNAH	BOO'-NA
BUNNI	BUNN'-EYE
BUZ	BUZZ'
BUZI	BUZZ'-EYE
BUZITE	BUZZ'-IGHT

–C–

CABBON	KABB'-ON
CABUL	KABB'-ELL
CAESAR	SEE'-ZAR
CAESAREA	SEZ-A-REE'-A
CAESAREA PHILIPPI	SEZ-A-REE'-A FILL'-IPP-EYE
CAIAPHAS	KYE'-A-FASS
CAIN	KEHN'

CAINAN	KEH'-NEN
CALAH	KAH'-LA
CALCOL	KAL'-KOL
CALEB	KEH'-LEB
CALEBITE	KEH'-LEB-IGHT
CHELUBAI	KE-LOO'-BUY
CALLISTHENES	KA-LISTH'-E-NEES
CALNEH	KAL'-NE
CALNO	KAL'-NO
CANNEH	KAN'-E
CALVARY	KAL'-VA-RE
CANA	KEH'-NA
CANAAN	KEH'-NAN
	KEH'-NA-AN
CANAANITES	KEHN'-AN-IGHTS
CANAANITESS	KEHN'-AN-IGHT-ESS
CANAANITISH	KEHN'-AN-IGHT-ISH
CANANAEAN	KAN'-A-NEE'-AN
CANDACE	KAN'-DA-SEE
CANNEH	KAN-E
CAPERNAUM	KA-PER'-NA-UMM
CAPHARSALAMA	KAF-AR-SAL'-E-MA
CAPHTOR	KAF'-TOR
CAPHTORIM	KAF'-TOR-IM
CAPPADOCIA	KAP-A-DOH'-SHA
CARABASION	KAR-A-BASS'-I-ON
CARCHEMISH	KAR-KEEM'-ISH
	KAR'-KEM-ISH
CARIA	KAR'-I-A
CARITES	KAR'-IGHTS
CARMEL	KAR'-MELL
CARMI	KAR'-MY
CARMITES	KAR'-MIGHTS
CARMONIANS	KAR-MOH'-NEE-ANS
CARNAIM	KAR'-NA-IM
KARNAIM	KAR-NAH'-EEM
CARPUS	KAR'-PUS
CARSHENA	KAR-SHEH'-NA
CASIPHIA	KASS-IF'-E-A
CASLUHIM	KASS'-LE-HIM
CASPIN	KASS'-PIN
CATHUA	KA-THOO'-A
CAUDA	KAW'-DA

27

CENCHREAE	KENG-KREE'-A
	SENG'-KRE-A
CENDEBEUS	KEN'-DE-BEE'-US
CEPHAS	CEE'-FASS
	KEH'-FASS
SIMON	SIGH'-MON
PETER	PEET'-ER
CHABRIS	KHAB'-RISS
CHADIASANS	KHA-DI-AS'-ANS
CHAEREAS	KHIR'-I-AS
CHALDEA	KAL-DEE'-A
CHALDEANS	KAL-DEE'-ANS
CHALPHI	KAL'-FIGH
CHAPHENATHA	KE-FEN'-E-THA
CHARAX	KAR'-AX
CHARMIS	KAR'-MISS
CHASPHO	KAS'-FOH
CHEBAR	KEE'-BAR
CHEDORLAOMER	KEDD'-ER-LA-OH'-MER
CHELAL	KEE'-LAL
CHELLEANS	KELL'-I-ANS
CHELOUS	KELL'-US
CHELUB	KEH'-LUBB
CHELUBAI	KI-LOO'-BUY
CHELUHI	KELL'-A-HIGH
CHEMOSH	KEE'-MOSH
CHENAANAH	KE-NAH'-A-NA
CHENANI	KE-NAH'-NIGH
CHENANIAH	KEN-EN-EYE'-A
CHEPHAR-AMMONI	KEE'-FAR-AM'-ON-EYE
CHERAN	KIRR'-AN
CHERETHITES	KER'-ETH-IGHTS
CHERITH	KER'-ITH
CHERUB	TCHER'-UBB
	KER-OOV'
CHERUBIM	TCHER'-U-BIMM
CHESALON	KESS'-A-LONN
CHESED	KEE'-SEDH
CHESIL	KEES'-ILL
CHESULLOTH	KE-SULL'-OTH
CHEZIB	KEE'-ZIV
CHIDON	KEE'-DON
CHILEAB	KILL'-I-AV

CHILION	KILL'-I-ON
CHILMAD	KILL'-MAD
CHIMHAM	KIM'-HAM
CHINNEROTH	KIN'-ER-OTH
CHINNERETH	KIN'-ER-ETH
CHIOS	KEE'-OSS
CHISLEV	KIZ'-LEV
CHISLON	KIS'-LON
CHISLOTH-TABOR	KIS'-LOTH-TEH'-BC
CHITLISH	KIT'-LISH
CHLOE	KLOH'-E
CHOBA	KOH'-BA
CHORAZIN	KOH-RADZ'-IN
CHORBE	KOR'-BE
CHUSI	KOO'-SI
CHUZA	KOO'-ZA
CILICIA	SILL-ISH'-A
CLAUDIA	KLAW'-DI-A
CLAUDIUS	KLAW-DI-US
CLEMENT	KLEM'-ENT
CLEOPAS	KLE'-OP-AS
CLEOPATRA	KLE-OP-AT'-RA
CLOPAS	KLOH'-PAS
CNIDUS	KNIGH'-DOS
COELE-SYRIA	KOIL'-EH-SEU'-RE-A
	SEEL'-EH-SIR'-I-A
COL-HOZEH	KOL-HOH'-ZE
COLOSSAE	KOL-OSS'-E
CONANIAH	KON'-AN-EYE'-A
JECONIAH	JEK-ON-EYE'-A
CONIAH	KOH-NIGH'-A
CORBAN	KOR'-BANN
CORINTH	KOR'-INTH
CORINTHIAN	KOR-INTH'-I-AN
CORNELIUS	KOR-NEEL'-I-US
COS	KOS'
COSAM	KOH'-SAM
COZBI	KOZZ'-BE
COZEBA	KOH-ZEE'-BA
CRESCENS	KRESS'-ENS
CRETE	KREET'
CRETANS	KREET'-ANS
CRISPUS	KRISS'-PUS

CUB	KUBB'
CUN	KUNN'
CUSH	KOOSH'
CUSHAN	KOOSH'-AN
CUSHAN-RISHATHAIM	KOOSH'-AN-RISH'-A-THA'-IMM
CUSHI	KOOSH'-EYE
CUSHITE	KOOSH'-IGHT
CUTH	KOOTH'
CUTHAH	KOOTH'-A
CUTHA	KOOTH'-A
CYAMON	SIGH'A-MON
CYPRUS	SIGH'-PRUSS
CYRENE	SIGH'-REE'-NE
CYRENIANS	SIGH-REEN'-I-ANS
CYRUS	SIGH'-RUSS
	KOO'-RUSS

– D –

DABBESHETH	DABB-ESH'-ETH
DABERATH	DA'-BER-ATH
DABRIA	DAB'-RE-A
DAGON	DEH'-GONN
	DAH-GOHN'
DALMANUTHA	DAL-MA-NOO'-THA
DALMATIA	DAL-MEH'-SHA
DALPHON	DAL'-FONN
DAMARIS	DAM'-AR-ISS
DAMASCUS	DAM'-ASK-US
DAN	DAN'
DANITE	DAN'-IGHT
DANIEL	DAN'-YELL
GAMAEL	GAM'-I-EL
DANNAH	DANN'-A
DAPHNE	DAF'-NE
DARDA	DAR'-DA
DARA	DAR'-A
DARIUS	DAR-EYE'-US
	DAR'-A-YA'-VA-HUSS
DARKON	DARK'-ON
DATHAN	DATH'-AN
DATHEMA	DATH'-EM-A
DAVID	DEH'-VIDD
	DAH'-WIDH
DEBIR	DE-VEER'
LO-DEBAR	LO-DEVAR

30

DEBORAH	DEB'-OR-A
	DE-BOHR'-A
DECAPOLIS	DE-CAP'-OLL-ISS
DEDAN	DEH'-DAN
DEDANITES	DEH'-DAN-IGHTS
DELAIAH	DE-LA'-YAH
DELILAH	DE-LIE'-LA
DELOS	DEE'-LOS
DEMAS	DEE'-MAS
DEMETRIUS	DE-MET'-RI-US
DERBE	DER'-BE
DESSAU	DESS'-O
DEUEL	DOO'-EL
DIANA	DYE-AN'-A
ARTEMIS	AR'-TEM-ISS
DIBLAIM	DIB'-LA-IM
DIBON	DYE'-BON
DIBON-GAD	DYE'-BON-GAD
DIBRI	DIB'-RYE
DIDYMUS	DID'-EM-US
DIKLAH	DIK'-LA
DILEAN	DILL'-E-AN
DIMNAH	DIM'-NA
DIMON	DYE'-MON
DIMONAH	DI-MOH'-NA
DINAH	DYE'-NA
DINHABAH	DINN'-HA-BA
DIONYSIUS	DYE-ON-ISH'-US
DIONYSUS	DYE-ON-EYE'-SUSS
DIOSCORINTHIUS	DEE'-OSS-KOR-IN'-THUSS
DIOTREPHES	DEE-OTT'-REF-EZ
DIPHATH	DYE'-FATH
DISHAN	DYE'-SHAN
DISHON	DYE'-SHON
DIVES	DYE'-VEES
DIZAHAB	DIZZ'-A-HAB
DODAI	DOH'-DYE
DODANIM	DOH'-DAN-IMM
DODAVAHU	DOH'-DA-VAH'-WHO
DODO	DOH'-DOH
DODAI	DOH'-DYE
DOEG	DOH'-IGG
DOK	DOCK'

DOPHKAH	DOFF'-KA
DORCAS	DOR'-KASS
DORYMENES	DOR-IMM'-EN-EZ
DOSITHEUS	DOS-ITH'-E-OSS
DOTHAN	DOH'-THANN
DRUSILLA	DROO-SILL'-A
DUMAN	DOO'-MA
DURA	DOO'-RA
DYSMAS	DIZZ'-MASS

— E —

EBAL	EE'BAL
EBED	EBB'-ED
EBED-MELECH	EBB'-ED-MEL'-EKH
EBENEZER	EEB'-BEN-EEZ'-ER
EBER	EE'-BER
EBEZ	EE'-BEZZ
EBIASAPH	EBB'-EE-EH'-SAF
EBRON	EBB'-RON
ECBATANA	EK-BAT'-EN-A
ECCLESIASTES	EK-KLEZ'-I-ASS'-TEASE
KOHELETH	KOH-HELL'-ETH
QOHELETH	KOH-HELL'-ETH
SOLOMON	SOL'-OM-ON
ECCLESIASTICUS	EK-KLEZ-I-AST'-I-CUSS
BEN SIRACH	BEN-SEE'-RACH
JESUS BEN SIRACH	JEEZ'-US-BEN-SEE'-RACH
EDEN	EE'-DEN
EDER	EE'-DER
EDNA	ED'-NA
EDOM	EE'-DOM
EDOMITES	EE'-DOM-IGHTS
IDUMEA	EYE-DEW-ME'-A
EDREI	ED'-RY
EGLAH	EGG'-LA
EGLAIM	EGG'-LE-EM
EGLATH-SHELISHIYAH	EGG'-LATH-SHEL-ISH'-I-YA
EGYPT	EE'-JIPT
EGYPTIAN	EDG-IP'-SHEN
EHI	EE'-HIGH
EHUD	EE'-HOOD
EKER	EE'-KER
EKRON	EK'-RON
EL	EHL'

32

ELA	EE'-LA
ELAH	EE'-LA
ELAM	EE'-LAM
ELAMITES	EE'-LAM-IGHTS
ELASA	ELL'-A-SA
ELASAH	ELL'-A-SA
ELATH	EE'-LATH
ELOTH	EE'-LOTH
EZION-GEBER	EZ'-I-ON-GHEE'-BER
EL-BERITH	ELL-BE-REETH'
EL-BETHEL	ELL-BETH'-ELL
ELDAAH	ELL-DAH'-A
ELDAD	ELL'-DAD
ELEAD	ELL'-I-ADD
ELEADAH	ELL-I-AH'-DA
ELEALEH	ELL-I-AH'-LE
ELEASAH	ELL-I-AH'-SA
ELEAZAR	ELL-I-EHZ'-ER
EL-ELOHE-ISRAEL	EL'-EL-OH'-HEH-IS'-RAH-EHL'
EL-ELYON	EHL'-ELL-YOHN'
ELEPHANTINE	EL-EF-ANT'-IN-E
ELEUTHERUS	E-LEUTH'-ER-US
ELHANAN	EL-HAH'-NAN
ELI	EE'-LIE
ELYON	ELL-YOHN'
ELI ELI LAMAH	EH'-LEE EH'-LEE LAM'-MA
SABACHTHANI	SA-BAKH-THAN'-NI
ELIJAH	ELL-EYE'-DJAH
	EH'-LEE-YA-HOO
ELOI	ELL-OH'-EE
ELIAB	E-LIE'-AB
ELIADA	E-LIE'-A-DA
ELIALIS	E-LIE'-A-LISS
ELIAM	EL-EYE'-AM
AMMIEL	AM'-E-EL
ELIASAPH	E-LIE'-A-SAF
ELIASHIB	E-LIE'-A-SHIBB
ELIASIS	E-LIE'-A-SISS
ELIATHAH	E-LIE'-A-THA
ELIDAD	E-LIE'-DAD
ELIEHOENAI	E-LIE'-E-HOH'-E-NIGH
ELIEL	E-LIE'-EL
ELIENAI	EL-I-EH'-NIGH

ELIEZER	EL-I-EH'-ZER
ELIEZAR	EL-I-EH-ZAR
ELIHOREPH	EL-I-HOHR'-EF
ELIHU	EL-EYE'-HEW
ELIAH	EL-EYE'-A
ELIJAH	EL-EYE'-DJAH
ELIKA	E-LIE'-KA
ELIM	EE'-LIMM
ELIMELECH	E-LIMM'-E-LEKH
ELIOENAI	ELL-I-OH-EH'-NIGH
ELIADAS	ELL-EYE'-A-DASS
ELIONAS	ELL-I-OH'-NASS
ELIPHAL	ELL-EYE'-FAL
ELIPHELET	ELL-IF'-A-LET
ELIPHAZ	ELL'-E-FAZ
ELIPHELEHU	ELL-IF'-EL-EH'-HOO
ELIPHELET	ELL-IF'-EL-ET
ELIPAHALAT	ELL-IF'-A-LAT
ELPELET	ELL-PEH'-LET
ELISHA	E-LIE'-SHA
ELISHAH	E-LIE'-SHA
ELISHAMA	E-LISH'-A-MA
ELISHAPHAT	E-LISH'-A-FAT
ELISHEBA	E-LISH'-E-BA
ELISHUA	E-LISH-OO'-A
ELIUS	E-LIE'-UDD
ELIZABETH	E-LIZ'-A-BETH
ELIZAPHAN	ELL-IZ-AH'-FAN
ELZAPHAN	ELL-ZAH'-FAN
ELIZUR	E-LIE'-ZER
ELKANAH	ELL-KAH'-NA
ELKIAH	ELL-KAI'-A
ELKOSH	ELL'-KOSH
ELLASAR	ELL'A-SAR
ELMADAM	ELL-MAH'-DAM
ELNAAM	ELL-NAH'-AM
ELNATHAN	ELL-NAH'-THANN
ELOI	ELL-OH'-EE
ELON	EE'-LON
ELONITES	EE'-LON-IGHTS
ELON-BETH-HANAN	EE'-LON-BETH-HAH'-NAN
ELOTH	EE'-LOTH
ELPAAL	ELL-PAH'-AL
EL-PARAN	ELL-PAH'-RENN

EL-SHADDAY	EL-SHAD'-DYE
ELTEKEH	ELL'-TE-KE
ELTEKE	ELL'-TE-KE
ELTEKON	ELL'-TE-KONN
ELTOLAD	ELL-TOH'-LAD
TOLAD	TOH'-LAD
ELUZAI	ELL-OOZE'-EYE
ELYMAIS	ELL-E-MAH'-ISS
ELYMAS	ELL'-E-MAS
BAR-JESUS	BAR-DJEES'-US
ELYON	EL-YOHN'
ELZABAD	ELL-ZAH'-BAD
ELZAPHAN	ELL-ZAH'-FAN
EMADABUN	E-MAD'-A-BEN
EMATHIS	EM'-A-THISS
ATHLAI	ATH'-LIE
EMIM	EH'-MIMM
EMMANUEL	EM-AH'-NOO-EL
EMMAUS	EM-EH'-US
ENAIM	E-NA'-IMM
ENAM	EH'-NAM
ENAN	EH'-NAN
ENDOR	EN'-DORR
EN-EGLAIM	EN-EGG'-LI-EM
EN-GANNIM	EN-GAN'-IMM
EN-GEDI	EN-GED'-I
EN-HADDAH	EN-HAD'-A
EN-HAKKORE	EN-HAKK'-ER-E
EN-HAZOR	EN-HEH'-ZOR
EN-MISHPAT	EN-MISH'-PAT
KADESH	KEH'-DESH
ENOCH	EE'-NOKH
ENOSH	EE'-NOSH
ENOS	EE'-NOSS
EN-RIMMON	EN-RIMM'-ON
AIN, RIMMON	EHN, RIMM'-ON
EN-ROGEL	EN-ROH'-GEL
EN-SHEMESH	EN-SHEM'-ESH
EN-TAPPUAH	EN-TAP'-YOO-A
EPAENETUS	EP-EYE'-NE-TUS
EPAPHRAS	E-PAF'-RAS
EPAPHRODITUS	E-PAF'-RO-DIE-TUS
EPHAH	EE'-FA
EPHAI	EE'-FIE

EPHER	EE'-FER
EPHES-DAMMIM	EE'-FES-DA-MEEM'
PAS-DAMMIN	PASS-DA'-MEEM'
EPHESUS	EF'-ES-US
EPHESIANS	EF-EES'-I-ANS
EPHLAL	EF'-LAL
EPHOD	EE'-FOD
EPHPHATHA	EF'-E-THA
EPHRAIM	EF'-RA-IM
EPHRAIMITE	EF'-RA-IMM-IGHT
EPHRATHAH	EF'-RATH-A
EPHRATH	EF'-RATH
BETHLEHEM EPHRATHAH	BETH'-LE-HEM EP'-RATH-A
EPHRATHITE	EF'-RA-THIGHT
EPICUREANS	EPI-KEW-REE'-ANS
EPIPHANES	E-PIFF'-AN-ES
ER	EHR'-
ERAN	EH'-RAN
ERASTUS	ER-AS'-TOS
ERECH	ER'-EKH
ERI	ER'-EYE
ERITES	ER'-IGHTS
ESARHADDON	EE'-SAR-HAD'-ON
ESAU	EE'-SAW
ESDRAELON	ES-DREH'-LON
JEZREEL	DJEZ-REEL'
	DJEZ'-REH-EL
ESDRAS	EZ'-DRAS
ESDRIS	EZ'-DRISS
ESEK	EE'-SEK
ESHAN	EE'-SHAN
ESHBAAL	ESH'-BA-AL
ISHBAAL	ISH'-BA-AL
ESHBAN	ESH'-BAN
ESHCOL	ESH'-KOHL
ESHEK	EE'-SHEK
ESHTAOL	ESH'-TE-OLL
ESHTAOLITES	ESH'-TE-OLL-IGHTS
ESHTEMOA	ESH'-TE-MOH'-A
ESHTEMOH	ESH'-TE-MOH
ESHTON	ESH'-TON
ESLI	EZ'-LIE
ESTHER	ESS'-TER
	ESS'-THER

36

ETAM	EE'-TAM
ETHAM	EE'-THAM
ETHAN	EE'-THANN
ETHBAAL	ETH'-BA-AL
ETHANUS	E-THAH'-NUS
ETHER	EE'-THER
ETHIOPIA	EE-THI-OH'-PIA
CUSH	KOOSH'
ETHIOPIANS	EE-THI-OH'-PI-ANS
ETH-KAZIN	ETH-KAH'-ZINN
ETHNAN	ETH'-NAN
ETHNARCH	ETH'-NARKH
ETHNI	ETH'-NIGH
EUBULUS	EU-BOOL'-US
EUCHARIST	EU'-KHAR-IST
	EU'-KAR-IST
EUERGETES	EU-ERG'-E-TES
EUMENES	EU'-MEN-EES
EUNICE	EU'-NISS
EUNUCH	EU'-NUKH
EUODIA	EU-OH'-DI-A
EUPHRATES	EU-FREH'-TEES
EUPOLEMUS	EU-POLL'-E-MUSS
EUROCLYDON	EUR-OKK'-LID-ON
EUTYCHUS	EU'-TIKH-US
EVANGELIST	EV-AN'-JEL-IST
EVE	EEV'
EVI	EE'-VIGH
EVIL-MERODACH	EH'VILL-MER'-A-DACH
EXODUS	EX'-ODD-USS
EZBAI	EZ'-BYE
EZBON	EZ'-BONN
EZEKHIEL	EZ-EEKH'-I-EL
EZEL	EE'-ZELL
EZEM	EE'-ZEMM
EZER	EE'-ZERR
EZION-GEBER	EZ'-I-ON - GHEE'-BERR
EZORA	E-ZOHR'-A
EZRA	EZ'-RA
EZRAHITE	EZ'-RA-HIGHT
EZRI	EZ'-RYE

–F–

[ANTONIUS] FELIX	[AN-TOH′-NI-US] FEE′-LICKS
[PORTIUS] FESTUS	[PORSCH′-I-US] FESS′-TUSS
FORTUNATUS	FOR-TEWN-EH′-TUSS
FORUM OF APPIUS	FOH′-RUMM OF APP′-I-US

–G–

GAAL	GEH′-AL
GAASH	GEH′-ASH
GABAEL	GAB′-A-EL
GABATHA	GAB′-A-THA
GABBAI	GA-BY′
GABBATHA	GAB′-A-THA
GABRIAS	GAB′-RI-AS
GABRIEL	GEH′-BRI-EL
GAD	GADD′
GADITE	GADD′-IGHT
[GADARA]	[GAD′-AR-A]
GADARENES	GAD′-AR-EENS
GADDI	GADD′-EYE
GADDIEL	GADD′-I-EL
GAHAM	GAH′-AM
GAHAR	GA′-HAR
GAI	GA′-EYE
GAIUS	GUY′-US
GALAL	GAL′-AL
GALATIA	GAL-EHSH′-A
GALATIANS	GAL-EHSH′-ANS
GAULS	GAWLS′
GALEED	GAL′-E-ED
GALILEE	GAL′-I-LEE
GALILEANS	GAL-I-LEE′-ANS
GALLIM	GALL′-IM
GALLIO [L. JUNIUS GALLIO	GAL′-I-O [YOU′-NE-US GAL′-I-C
ANNAEUS]	ANN-E′-US]
GAMAD	GAH′-MAD
GAMAEL	GAM′-A-EL
DANIEL	DAN′I-EL
GAMALIEL	GAM-EH′-LI-EL
GAMUL	GAH′-MULL
GAREB	GEH′-REB
GARMITE	GAR′-MIGHT
GATAM	GAH′-TAM

GATH	GATH'
GITTITE	GIT'-IGHT
GATH-HEPHER	GATH-HEE'-FER
GATH-RIMMON	GATH-RIMM'-ON
GAULANITIS	GO'-LAN-IGHT'-ISS
GOLAN IN BASHAN	GO'-LAN-IN-BEH'-SHAN
GAUL	GAWL'
GAULS	GAWLS'
GALATIANS	GAL-EH'-SHENS
GAZA	GAH'-ZA / GEH'-ZA
GAZAITES	GAH'-ZA-IGHTS/GEH'-ZA-IGHTS
GAZARA	GAZ'-A-RA
GEZER	GEEZ'-ER
GAZEZ	GEH'-ZEZ
GEBA	GEEB'-A
GEBAL	GEEB'-AL
GEBALITES	GEEB'-AL-IGHTS
BYBLOS	BIBB'-LOSS
GEBER	GEEB'-ER
GEBIM	GEEB'-IM
GEDALIAH	GEDD-A-LIE'-A
GEDER	GEED'-ER
GEDERITE	GEED'-ER-IGHT
GEDERAH	GIDD-IRR'-A
GEDEROTH	GE-DIRR'-OTH
GEDEROTHAIM	GE-DIRR'-OTH-AH'-IM
GEDOR	GEED'-OR
GE-HARASHIM	GE-HARR'-A-SHIMM
GEHAZI	GE-HEHZ'-EYE
GEHENNA	GE-HENN'-A
GE-HINNOM	GEH'-HINN-OHM
HADES	HEH'-DEES
GELILOTH	GE-LIE'-OTH
GEMALLI	GE-MALL'-E
GEMARIAH	GE-MAR-EYE'-A
GENESIS	JEN'-E-SISS
GENNAEUS	GE-NIGH'-US
GENNESARET	GE-NESS'-AR-ET
GENUBATH	GE-NOO'-BATH
GERA	GIRR'-A
GERAR	GIRR'-AR
[GERASA]	[GER'-A-SA]
GERASENES	GER'-A-SEENS
[JERASH]	[JER'-ASH]

GERIZIM	GER'-I-ZIM
GERSHOM	GER'-SHOMM
GERSHOMITES	GER-SHAMM-IGHTS
GERUTH CHIMHAM	GE'-ROOTH-KIMM'-HAM
GESHAN	GESH'-AN
GESHEM	GESH'-EM
GESHUR	GESH'-ER
GESHURITES	GESH'-ER-IGHTS
GETHER	GEETH'-ER
GETHSEMANE	GETH-SEM'-A-NE
GESAMINI	GEH-SAM'-I-NE
GEUEL	GOO'-EL
GEZER	GEEZ'-ER
GIAH	GYE'-A
GIBBAR	GIBB'-AR
GIBBETHON	GIBB'-ETH-ON
GIBEA	GIBB'-E-A
GIBEATH	GIBB'-E-A
GIBEATH-ELOHIM	GIBB'-E-ATH-EL-OH'-HEMM
GIBEATH-HA-ARALOTH	GIBB'-E-ATH-HA-AHR'-AL-OTH
GIBEON	GIBB'-E-ON
GIBEONITES	GIBB'-E-ON-IGHTS
GIDDALTI	GIDD-ALT'-EYE
GIDDEL	GIDD'-EL
GIDEON	GIDD'-E-ON
JERUBBAAL	JER-UB-BA-AL
GIDEONI	GIDD-E-OHN'-EYE
GIDOM	GIDD'-OMM
GIHON	GUY'-HON
	GI'-HOHN
GILALAI	GI-LAH'-LI
GILBOA	GIL-BOH'-A
GILEAD	GIL'-E-AD
GILEADITES	GIL'-E-ADD-IGHTS
GILGAL	GIL'-GAL
GILOH	GUY'-LO
GILO	GUY'-LO
GILONITE	GUY'-LON-IGHT
GIMZO	GIM'-ZO
GINATH	GUY'-NATH
GINNETHOI	GINN'-ETH-OI
GINNETHON	GINN'-ETH-ON
GIRGASHITE	GIRR'-GASH-IGHT

GIRZITES	GIRR'-ZIGHTS
GIZRITES	GIZZ'-RIGHTS
GISHPA	GISH'-PE
GITTAIM	GITT'-I-EM
GITTITE	GITT'-IGHT
GIZONITE	GUY'-ZONN-IGHT
HASHEM	HASH'-EM
GOAH	GO'-A
GOB	GOBB'
	GOHB'
GOG	GOGG'
MAGOG	MAH'-GOGG
GOIIM	GOY'-EEM
GOLGOTHA	GOL'-GOTH-A
GOLIATH	GOL-EYE'-ATH
GOMER	GOH'-MER
GOMORRAH	GE-MORR'-A
GORGIAS	GORG'-I-AS
GORTYNA	GOR-TEE'NA
GORTYN	GOR'-TIN
GOSHEN	GOH'-SHEN
GOTHOLIAH	GOTH-AL-EYE'-A
ATHALIAH	ATH-AL-EYE'-A
GOTHONIEL	GOH-THON'-I-EL
GOZAN	GOH'-ZAN
GREECE [HELLAS]	GREES'- [HELL'ASS]
GREEK	GREEK'
GREEKS [HELLENES]	GREEKS' [HELL'-EENS]
GUDGODAH	GUDH-GOH'-DA
HOR-HAGGIDAD	KHOR'-HA-GIDD'-AD
GUNI	GOON'-EYE
GUNITES	GOON'-IGHTS
GUR	GOOR'
GURBAAL	GOOR'-BAH'-AL
GYMNASIUM	JIM-NEH-SI-UM
GYMNASIA	JIM-NEH-SI-A

– H –

HAAHASTARI	HAH'-E-HASH'-TA-RI
AHASHTARITES	A-HASH'-TER-IGHTS
HABAIAH	KHA-BUY'-A
HOBAIAH	KHOH-BUY'-A
HABAKKUK	HAB'-A-KOOK
	KHA-BAKK'-OOK

HABAZZINIAH	HABB-A-ZINN-EYE'-A
HABIRU	HAH'-BI-ROO
HAPIRU	HAH'-PI-ROO
HEBREW	HEE'-BREW
HABOR	HEH'-BOR
HACHILAH	HA-KEE'-LA
HACHMONI	HAKH-MOH'-NI
HACHMONITE	HAKH'-MON-IGHT
HADAD	HEH'-DAD
HADADEZER	HAD-A-DEEZ'-ER
HADADRIMMON	HEH'-DAD-RIMM'-ON
HADAR	HEH'-DAR
HADAD	HEH'-DAD
HADASHAH	HA-DASH'-A
HADASSAH	HA-DASS'-A
HADES	HEH'-DEES
GEHENNA	GE-HEN'-A
HADID	HEH'-DID
HADLAI	HAD'-LIE
HADORAM	HA-DOHR'-AM
HADRACH	HAD'-RAKH
HA-ELEPH	HA-EL'-EF
HAGAB	HAG'-AB
HAGABAH	HAG'-AB-A
HAGABA	HAG'-AB-A
HAGAR	HEH'-GAR
HAGGAI	HAG'-EYE
	HAG'-EH-EYE
HAGGEDOLIM	HAG-ED-OHL'-IM
HAGGI	HAG'-GY
HAGGITES	HAG'-IGHTS
HAGGIAH	HAG-EYE'-A
HAGGITH	HAG'-ITH
HAGRI	HAG'-RYE
HAGRITE	HAG'-RIGHT
HAHIROTH	HA-HY'-ROTH
PI-HAHIROTH	PY'-HA-HY'-ROTH
HAKKOZ	HAK'-OHS
ACCOS	AKK'-OSS
HAKUPHA	HA-KOO'-FA
HALAH	HA'-LA
HALAK	HA'-LAKK
HALHUL	HAL'-HULL
HALI	HAH'-LIE

HALICARNASSUS	HAL-I-KAR-NASS'-US
HALLEL	HAL'-EL
HALLELUJAH	HAL'-EL-EU'YA
ALLELUIA	AL'-EL-EU'-YA
HALLOHESH	HA-LOH'-HESH
HAM	HAM'
HAMITES	HAM'-IGHTS
HAMAN	HEH'-MAN
HAMATH	HAM'-ATH
HAMATHITE	HAM'-ATH-IGHT
HAMATH-ZOBAH	HAM'-ATH-ZOH'-BA
ZOBAH	ZOH'-BA
HAMMATH	HAM'-ATH
HAMMEDATHA	HAM'-ED-AH'-THA
HAMMOLECHETH	HAM-OLL'-EKH-ETH
HAMMON	HAM'-ON
HAMMOTH-DOR	HAM'-OTH-DOHR'
HAMMUEL	HAM'-EW-EL
HAMMURABI	HAM'-URR-RA'-BI
AMRAPHEL	AM'-RA-FELL
HAMONAH	HAM-OH'-NA
HAMON-GOG	HA'-MON-GOG'
HAMOR	HA'-MOHR
HAMRAN	HAM'-RAN
HEMDAN	HEM'-DAN
HAMUL	HA'-MUL
HAMUTAL	HA-MOO'-TAL
HANAMEL	HAN'-A-MEL
HANANEL	HAN'-A-NEL
HANANI	HA-NAH'-NI
HANANIAH	HAN'-AN-EYE'-A
HANES	HA'-NIZZ
HANNAH	HAN'-NA
HANNATHON	HAN'-A'-THON
HANNIEL	HAN'-I-EL
HANOCH	HAN'-OKH
HANOCHITES	HAN'-OKH-IGHTS
HANUKKAH	KHAN'-UKH-A
HANUN	KHAN'-UN
HAPHARIM	HAF'-AR-IM
HAPPIZZEZ	HAP-IZ'-EZ
HARA	HAH'-RA
HARADAH	HA-RAH'-DA
HARAN	HA-RAHN'

HARARITE	HAR'-AR-IGHT
HARBONA	HAR-BOH'-NA
HAREPH	HAH'-REF
HARHAIAH	HAR-HAH'-YA
HARHAS	HAR'-HAS
HARHUR	HAR'-HUR
	HAR'-HURR
HAR-HERES	HAR-HER'-EZ
HARIM	HAR'-IMM
HARIPH	HAR'-IF
HARMON	HAR'-MON
HARNEPHER	HAR-NEF'-ER
HAROD	HAR'-ODD
HARODITE	HAR'-ODD-IGHT
HAROEH	HA-ROH'-E
REAIAH	RE-EYE'-A
HAROSHETH-HAGOIIM	HA-ROSH'-ETH-HA-GOY'-IM
HARSHA	HAR'-SHA
CHAREA	KHAR'-E-A
HARUM	HAR'-UM
HARUMAPH	HA-ROOM'-AF
HARUPHITE	HA-ROOF'-IGHT
SHEPHATIAH	SHEF-AT-EYE'-A
HARUZ	KHAR'-UZ
HASADIAH	HAS-A-DYE'-A
HASHABIAH	HASH-A-BUY'-A
ASIBIAS	ASS-IBB'-I-AS
HASHABNAH	HA-SHABB'-NA
HASHABNEIAH	HA-SHABB-NYE'-A
HASHBADDANAH	HASH-BAD'-A-NA
HASHEM	HAH'-SHEM
HASHMONAH	HASH-MOH'-NA
HASHUBAH	HA-SHOO'-BA
HASHUM	HASH'-UM
HASIDEANS	KHAS-ID'-E-ANS
HASIDIM	KHS'-ID-EEM
HASMONEUS	HASS-MOHN'-E-US
HASMONEANS	HASS-MONN-E'-ANS
HASRAH	HAS'-RA
HARHAS	HAR'-HASS
HASSENAAH	HASS-EN-AH'-A
SENAAH	SEN-AH'-A
HASSENOAH	HASS-E-NOO'-A
HASSHUB	HASH'-UBB

HASSOPHERETH	HASS-OH'-FER-ETH
SOPHERETH	SOH'-FER-ETH
HATHACH	HAH'-THAKH
HATHATH	HAH'-THATH
HATIPHA	HAT-EYE'-FA
HATITA	HAT-EYE'-TA
HATTIL	HAT'-ILL
HATTUSH	HAT'-USSH
HAURAN	HOH'-RAN
HAVILAH	HAV'-ILL-A
HAVVOTH-JAIR	HAV'-OTH-YAH'-EER
HAZAEL	HA'-ZE-EL
HAZAIAH	HA-ZA'-YAH
HAZAR-ADDAR	HAZ'-AR-ADD'-ER
HAZAR-ENAN	HAZ'-AR-EE'-NAN
HAZAR-ENON	HAZ'-AR-EE'-NON
HAZAR-GADDAH	HAZ'-AR-GADD'-A
HAZARMAVETH	HAZ'-AR-MAH'-VITH
HAZAR-SHUAL	HAZ'-AR-SHOO'-AL
HAZAR-SUSAH	HAZ'-AR-SOO'-SA
HAZAR-SUSIM	HAZ'-AR-SOO'-SEEM
HAZAZON-TAMAR	HAZ'-A-ZON-TAH'-MAR
HAZER-HATTICON	HAZ'-ER-HAT'-I-KON
HAZEROTH	HAZ'-ER-OTH
HAZIEL	HAZ'-I-EL
HAZO	HAZ'-OH
HAZOR	HEH'-ZOR
	HA'-ZOHR
HAZOR-HADATTAH	HAZ'-OR-HA-DATT'-A
HAZZELELPONI	HAZ'-A-LEL-POH'-NIGH
HEBER	HE'-BER
HEBERITES	HE'-BER-IGHTS
HEBER	HE'-BER
EBER	EE'-BER
HEBREW	HE'-BREW
HEBRON	HE'-BRON
	HEV-ROHN'
HEBRONITES	HE'-BRON-IGHTS
HEGAI	HEG'-EYE
HEGEMONIDES	HEG-E-MON'-I-DEES
HEGLAM	HEG'-LAM
HELAH	HE'-LAH
HELAM	HE'-LAM
HELBAH	HEL'-BA

HELBON	HEL'-BON
HELDAI	HEL'-DYE
HELEB	HEL'-EBB
HELED	HEL'-ED
HELECH	HEL'-EKH
HELEK	HEL'-EK
HELEKITES	HEL'-EK-IGHTS
HELEPH	HEL'-EFF
HELEM	HEL'-EM
HELER	HEL'-ER
HELEZ	HEL'-EZ
HELI	HEE'-LIE
ELI	EE'-LIE
HELIODORUS	HEL-I-O-DOHR'-US
HELIOPOLIS	HEL-I-OPP'-O-LIS
HELKAI	HELK'-EYE
HELKATH	HEL'-KATH
HUKOK	HOO'-KOK
HELKATH-HAZZURIM	HEL'-KATH-HAZ'-OOR-IM
HELLENISTS	HELL'-EN-ISTS
HELON	HEL'-ON
HEMAM	HEH'-MAM
HOMAM	HOH'-MAM
HEMAN	HEH'-MAN
HEMDAN	HEM'-DAN
HENA	HEN'-NA
HENADAD	HEN'-A-DAD
HEPHER	HEE'-FER
HEPHERITES	HEE'-FER-IGHTS
HEPHZIBAH	HEF'-ZI'-BA
HERCULES	HER'-KEW-LEES
HERES	HER'-ES
HERESH	HER'-ESH
HERETH	HER'-ETH
HERMOGENES	HER-MOJ'-EN-EES
HERMON	HER'-MON
HERMONITES	HER'-MON-IGHTS
HEROD	HER'-OD
HERODIANS	HER-OHD'-I-ANS
HERODIAS	HER-OHD'-I-ASS
HESHBON	HESH'-BON
HESHMON	HESH'-MON
HETH	HETH'
HETHLON	HETH'-LON

HEZEKIAH	HEZ-EK-EYE'-A
HEZION	HEZ'-I-ON
HEZIR	HEZ'-EER
HEZRO	HEZ'-ROH
HEZRON	HEZ'-RON
HEZRONITES	HEZ'-RON-IGHTS
HIDDAI	HID'-EYE
HURAI	HOOR'-EYE
HIDDEKEL	HID'-E-KELL
TIGRIS	TIE'-GRISS
HIEL	HY'-EL
HIERAPOLIS	HE'-ER-A'-POL-ISS
HIERONYMUS	HE'-ER-ON'-I-MUS
HILEN	HIGH'-LEN
HILKIAH	HILL-KYE'-A
HILLEL	HILL'-EL
HINNOM	HINN'-OHM
GEHENNA	GE-HENN'-A
HIPPOPOTAMUS	HIPP'-O-POT'-A-MUS
BEHEMOTH	BEE'-HE-MOTH
	BE-HEH'-MOHT
HIRAH	HIGH'-RA
HIRAM	HIGH'-RAM
HITTITES	HITT'-IGHTS
HIVITES	HIVV'-IGHTS
HIZKI	HITS'-KY
HIZKIAH	HITS-KY'-A
HOBAB	KHOH'-BAB
HOBAH	KHOH'-BA
HOBAIH	KHOB-EYE'-A
HOD	KHOHD'
HODAVIAH	HOD-AV-EYE'-A
HODEVAH	HOH'-DE-VAH
HODESH	KHOH'-DESH
HODEVAH	HOH'-DE-VA
HODIAH	HOD'-EYE-A
HOGLAH	KHOG'-LA
HOLOFERNES	HOL-O-FER'-NEES
HOLON	KHOH'-LON
HOMAN	HOH'-MAM
HOPHNI	HOF'-NI
HOPHRA	HOFF'-RA
HOR	HOHR'
HORAM	HOHR'-AM

HOREB	HOR'-EB
	KHOH'-REB
SINAI	SIGH'-NYE
	SEE'-NYE
HOREM	KHOHR'-EM
HOR-HAGGIDAD	KHOHR'-HA-GIDD'-AD
GUDGODAH	GUDH-GOHD'-A
HORI	HOHR'-EYE
HORITES	HOHR'-IGHTS
HORMAH	KHOR'-MA
HORONAIM	KHOHR'-ON-AH'-IM
HORONITE	KHOR'-ON-IGHT
HOSAH	KHOH'-SA
HOSANNA	HOHZ-ANN'-A
HOSEA	HOHZ-EE'-A
	HOHZ-EH'-A
HOSHAIAH	HOH-SHAH'-YA
HOSHAMA	HOH-SHAH'-MA
HOSHEA	HOH-SHE'-A
HOTHAM	KHOH'-THAM
HOTHIR	KHOH'-THER
HOZAI	KHOHZ'-EYE
HUKKOK	HUKK'-OKK
HUKOK	HOOK'-OKK
HUL	HOOL'
HULDAH	HULL'-DA
HUMTAH	KHUMM'-TA
HUPHAM	HOO'-FAM
HUPPIM	HUPP'-IM
HUPHAMITES	HOO'-FAM-IGHTS
HUPPAH	KHUPP'-A
HUPPIM	HUPP'-IM
HUPHAM	HOO'-FAM
HURAI	KHOO'-RYE
HIDDAI	KHID'-EYE
HURAM	KHUR'-AM
HURAMABI	KHUR'-AM-AB'-I
HIRAM	HIGH'-RAM
HURI	KHUR'-EE
HURRIANS	HURR'-I-ANS
HORITES	HOH'-RIGHTS
HUSHAH	HOOSH'-A
HUSHATHITE	HOOSH'-A-THIGHT
HUSHAI	HOO'-SHY

HUSHIM	HOO'-SHIMM
HYDASPES	HIGH-DASS'-PES
HYKSOS	HIKK'-SOSS
HYMENAEUS	HIGH'-MEN-EE'-US
HYRCANUS	HIRR-CAN'-US

—I—

IBHAR	IBB'-HAR
IBLEAM	IBB'-LI-AM
IBNEIAH	IBB-NIGH'-YA
IBNIJAH	IBB'-NI-YA
IBRI	IBB'-RYE
IBSAM	IBB'-SAM
IBZAN	IBB'-ZAN
ICHABOD	IK'-A-BODD
	EEKH'-AV-ODH
ICONIUM	EYE-KOHN'-I-UM
IDALAH	IDD'-A-LA
IDBASH	ID'-BASH
IDDO	IDD'-OH
IDUEL	ID-OO'-EL
ARIEL	AR'-I-EL
IDUMEA	EYE'-DO-MEE'-A
EDOM	EE'-DOM
IEZER	EE-EHZ'-ER
IEZERITES	EE-EHZ'-ER-IGHTS
ABIEZER	AB'-EE-EHZ-ER
IGAL	EYE'-GAL
IGDALIAH	IGG-DAL-EYE'-AH
IIM	EYE'-YIMM
IJON	EYE'-YONN
IKKESH	IKK'-ESH
ILAI	EYE'-LIE
ILIADUN	ILL'-E-A-DUN
ILLYRICUM	ILL-IRR'-I-CUMM
IMALKUE	IMM-AHL'-KOO-E
IMLAH	IMM'-LA
IMMANUEL	IMM-AN'-OO-EL
	IMM-AN'-YEW-EL
EMMANUEL	EMM-AN'-YEW-EL
IMMER	IMM'-ER
IMNA	IMM'-NA
IMNAH	IMM'-NA

49

IMRAH	IMM'-RA
IMRI	IMM'-RYE
INDIA	IND-E-A
	IN'-DJA
IOB	JOHB'
IOTA	EYE-OH'-TA
IPHEIAH	IF-EE'-YA
IPHTAH	IF'-TA
IPHTAH-EL	IF'-TA-EL
IR	EYR'
IRA	EYE'-RA
IRAD	EYE'-RADD
IRAM	EYE'-RAM
IRI	EYR'-RYE
IRIJAH	IRR-EYE'-JAH
IRPEEL	IRR'-PE-EL
IR-SHEMESH	IRR-SHEM'-ISH
IRU	EYE'-ROO
ISAAC	EYE'-ZAKK
ISAIAH	EYE-ZEH'-A
	EYE-ZY'-A
JESHAIAH	YE-SHA'-YAH
[ISHBAAL]	[ISH'-BA-AL]
ESHBAAL	ESH'-BA-AL
ISHBOSHETH	ISH-BOSH'-ETH
ISHBAH	ISH'-BA
ISHBAK	ISH'-BAKK
ISHBI-BENOB	ISH'-BY-BEE'-NOB
ISHBOSHETH	ISH-BOSH'-ETH
ESHBAAL	ESH'-BA-AL
[ISHBAAL]	[ISH'-BA-AL]
ISH-HAI	ISH'-HY
ISHHOD	ISH'-HODD
ISHI	YISH'-EYE
	ISH'-EYE
ISHMAEL	ISH'-MEHL
	ISH'-MA-EL
	YISH'-MA-EL
ISHMAELITES	ISH'-MEH-LIGHTS
ISHMAIAH	ISH-MEH'-YA
ISHMERAI	ISH'-MER-EYE
ISHPAH	ISH'-PA
ISHPAN	ISH'-PAN
ISHVAH	ISH'-VA

ISHVI	ISH'-VY
ISHVITES	ISH'-VIGHTS
ISHMACHIAH	ISS-MAKH-EYE'-A
ISRAEL	IZ'-REHL
	IS-RA-EL
ISRAELITES	IZ'-REH-LIGHTS
ISSACHAR	ISS'-AKH-AR
ISSHIAH	ISH-EYE'-YA
ISSHIJAH	ISH-EYE'-YA
ISTALCURUS	ISS-TALL'-KOO-ROSS
ITALY	IT'-A-LE
ITALIAN COHORT	IT-AL'-I-AN KOH'-HORT
ITHAI	ITH'-EYE
ITHAMAR	ITH'-A-MAR
ITHIEL	ITH'-I-EL
ITHLAH	ITH'-LA
ITHMAH	ITH'-MA
ITHNAN	ITH'-NAN
ITHRA	ITH'-RA
ITHRAN	ITH'-RAN
ITHREAM	ITH'-RE-AM
ITHRITES	ITH'-RIGHTS
ITTAI	IT'-EYE
ITURAEA	IT'-YOO-REE'-A
IVVAH	IVV'-A
IYE-ABARIM	EYE'-YA-AB'-A-RIM
IYIM	EYE'-YIM
IZHAR	IZ'-HAR
IZHARITES	IZ'-HA-RIGHTS
IZLIAH	IZ-LIE'-A
IZRAHIAH	IZ-RA-HIGH'-YA
IZRAHITE	IZ'-RA-HIGHT
IZRI	IZ'-RY
IZZIAH	IZ-EYE'-YA

–J–

JAAKAN	JA'-A-KAN
JAAKOBAH	JA'-A-KOH'-BA
JAALA	JA'-A-LA
JAALAH	JEH'-A-LA
JAAR-OREGIM	JA'-AR-I-OHR'-E-GHIM
JAARESHIAH	JAR'-E-SHY'-YA
JAASIEL	JA-AS'-I-EL

51

JAASU	JA'-A-SOO
JAAZANIAH	JA-AZ'-A-NIGH'-YA
JEZANIAH	JEZ'-A-NIGH'-YA
JAAZIAH	JA'-AZ-EYE'-YA
JAAZIEL	JA-AZ'-I-EL
AZIEL	AZ'-I-EL
JABAL	JA'-BAL
JABBOK	JAB'-BOK
JABESH	JEH'-BISH
JABESH-GILEAD	JEH'-BISH-GILL'-I-AD
JABEZ	JEH'-BEZZ
JABIN	JEH'-BINN
JABNEEL	JAB'-NI-EL
JABNEH	JAB'-NE
JAMNIA	JAM'-NI-A
JABNEH	JAB'-NE
JABNEEL	JAB'-NE-EL
JACAN	JEH'-KAN
JACHIN	JEH'-KIN
JACHINITES	JEH'-KIN-IGHTS
JACOB	JEH'-KOBB
ISRAEL	IZ'-REHL
	IZ'-RA-EL
JADA	JA'-DA
JADDAI	JADD'-EYE
JADDUA	JADD-OO'-A
JADDUS	JADD'-US
JADON	JA'-DON
JAEL	JEHL'
JAH	JAH'
YAH	YAH'
JAHATH	JA'-HATH
JAHAZ	JA'-HAZZ
JAHZAH	JA'-ZA
JAHAZIEL	JE-HAZ'-I-EL
JAHDAI	JA'-DYE
JAHDIEL	JA'-EI-EL
JAHDO	JA'-DOH
JAHLEEL	JA'-LI-EL
JAHLEELITES	JA'-LI-EL-IGHTS
JAHMAI	JA'-MY
JAHVEH	JAH'-VE
YAHWEH	YAH'-WAY
JAHZAH	JA'-ZA

JAHZEEL	JAZZ'-I-EL
JAHZEELITES	JAZZ'-I-EL-IGHTS
JAHZIEL	JAZZ'-I-EL
JAHZEIAH	JAZZ-EH'-YAH
JAHZERAH	YAH'-ZE'-RA
JAHZIEL	JAZZ'-I-EL
JAIR	JA'-EER
JAIRITE	JA'-IR-IGHT
JAIRUS	JEH'-RUSS
	JEH-IR-US
JAKEH	JA'-KE
JAKIM	JA'-KIM
JALAM	JA'-LAM
JALON	JA'-LON
JAMBRES	JAM'-BRES
JAMBRI	JAM'-BRY
JAMES	JEHMS'
JACOB	JAY'-KOBB
JAMIN	JA'-MINN
JAMINITES	JA'-MINN-IGHTS
JAMLECH	JAM'-LEKH
JAMNIA	JAM'-NI-A
JANAI	JA'-NYE
JANIM	JANN'-IM
JANNAI	JANN'-EYE
JANNES	JANN'-EZ
JANNEUS	JANN-E'-US
ALEXANDER	AL-EX-AN'-DER
JANOAH	JA-NOH'-A
JAPHETH	JAFF'-ETH
JAPHIA	JA-FY'-A
JAPHLET	JAF'-LET
JAPHLETITES	JAF'-LET-IGHTS
JARAH	JA'-RA
JARED	JAR'-ED
JARHA	JAR'-HA
JARIB	JAR'-IB
JARMUTH	JAR'-MUTH
JAROAH	JA-ROH'-A
JASHAR	JASH'-AR
JASHEN	JASH'-EN
JASHOBEAM	JA-SHOH'-BE-AM
JASHUB	JASH'-UBB
JASHUBITES	JASH'-UBB-IGHTS

JASON	JEH'-SONN
JATHAN	JA'-THAN
JATHNIEL	JATH'-NI-EL
JATTIR	JATT'-IRR
JAVAN	JA'-VAN
JAZER	JAZZ'-ER
JAZIZ	JAZZ'-IZ
JEARIM	JE'-AR-IM
JEATHERAI	JE-ATH'-ER-EYE
JEBERECHIAH	JEBB-ER'-EKH-EYE'-YA
JEBUS	JEE'-BUS
JEBUSITE	JEB'-BUS-IGHT
	JEB'-YEW-SIGHT
JECHONIAH	JEKH-O-NY'-YA
JECOLIAH	JEKH-O-LIE'-YA
JECONIAH	JEKH-ON'-YA
JEDAIAH	JED-A'-YA
JEDIAEL	JE-DIE'-EL
JEDIDAH	JE-DIE'-DA
JEDIDIAH	JE-DID-EYE'-YA
JEDUTHUN	JE-DOO'-THUN
JEGAR-SAHADUTHA	JE'-GAR-SA'-HA-DOO'-TH.
JEHALLELEL	JE-HAL'-EL-EL
JEHDEIAH	JE-DY'-YA
JEHEZKEL	JE-HEZ'-KEL
JEHIAH	JE-HIGH'-YA
JEHIEL	JE-HIGH'-EL
JEHUEL	JE-HOO'-EL
JEHIELI	JE-HIGH'-EL-EYE
JEHOADDAH	JE-HOH'-A-DA
JEHOADDAN	JE-HOH'-A-DAN
JEHOADDIN	JE-HOH'-A-DIN
JEHOAHAZ	JE-HOH'-A-HAZ
JOAHAZ	JOH'-A-HAZ
JEHOASH	JE-HOH'-ASH
JEHOHANAN	JE-HOH'-AN-AN
JEHOIACHIN	JE-HOI'-AKH-IN
JECONIAH	JEKH-ON'-YAH
CONIAH	KOHN'-YAH
JECHONIAH	JEKH-ON'-YAH
JEHOIADA	JE-HOI'-A-DA
JEHOIAKIM	JE-HOI'-YA-KIM
JEHOIARIB	JE-HOI'-YA-RIB
JEHONADAB	JE-HON'-A-DAB

54

JEHONATHAN	JE-HON'-ATH-AN
JEHORAM	JE-HOH'-RAM
JEHOSHABEATH	JE-HOH-SHAB'-E-ATH
JEHOSHEBA	JE-HOSH'-E-BA
JEHOSHAPHAT	JE-HOSH'-E-FAT
JOSHAPHAT	JOSH'-A-FAT
JEHOSHEBA	JE-HOSH'-E-BA
JEHOSHABEATH	JE-HOH-SHAB'-E-ATH
JEHOZABAD	JE-HOHZ'-A-BAD
JEHU	JEE'-HOO
JEHUBBAH	JE-HUBB'-A
JEHUCAL	JE-HUKH'-AL
JUCAL	JUKH'-AL
JEHUD	JE'-HOOD
JEHUDI	JE-HOOD'-EYE
JEHUEL	JE'-HOO-EL
JEIEL	JE-EYE'-EL
OCHIEL	OKH'-I-EL
JEKABZEEL	JE-KAB'-ZE-EL
KABZEEL	KAB'-ZE-EL
JEKAMEAM	JE-KAM'-E-AM
JEKAMIAH	JE-KAM-EYE'-YA
JEKUTHIEL	JE-KOOTH'-I-El
JEMIMAH	JE-MY'-MA
JEMUEL	JEM'-OO-EL
JEPHTHAH	JEF'-THA
JEPHUNNEH	JE-FUNN'-A
JERAH	JE'-RA
JERAHMEEL	JE-RA'-ME-EL
JERAHMEELITE	JE-RA'-ME-EL-IGHT
JEREMIEL	JE-REM'-E-EL
JERED	JER'-ED
JEREMAI	YER'-E-MY
JEREMIAH	JER-EM-EYE'-YA
JEREMIEL	JE-REM'-E-EL
JEREMOTH	JE'-REM-OTH
JERIMOTH	JE'-RIM-OTH
JERIAH	JE-RYE'-YA
JERIJAH	JE-RYE'-JA
JERIBAI	JER'-I-BY
JERICHO	JER'-I-HOH
JERIEL	JER'-I-EL
JERIJAH	JE-RYE'-JA
JERIAH	JE-RYE'-YA

JERIMOTH	JE'-RIM-OTH
JEREMOTH	JE-REM-OTH
JERIOTH	JER'-I-OTH
JEROBOAM	JER-O-BOH'-AM
JEROHAM	JER-OH'-HAM
JERUBBAAL	JER-UBB'-BA-AL
	JER'-UBB-BA-AL
JERUBBESHETH	JER'-UBB-BESH'-ETH
JERUEL	JE-ROO'-EL
JERUSALEM	JE-ROO'-SA-LEM
JERUSHA	JE-ROO'-SHA
JERUSHAH	JE-ROO'-SHA
JESHAIAH	JE-SHA'-YA
JESHANAH	JE-SHA'-NA
JESHARELAH	JE-SHAR-EHL'-A
JESHEBEAB	JE-SHEB'-E-AB
JESHER	JE'-SHER
JESHIMON	JESH-EYE'-MON
JESHISHAI	JE-SHISH'-EYE
JESHUA	JESH-OO'-A
JOSHUA	JOSH'-OO-A
JESHURUN	JESH'-URR-UNN
JESIMIEL	JE-SIMM-EYE'-EL
JESSE	JESS'-E
JESUS	JEEZ'-US
JETHER	JEE'-THER
JETHETH	JEE'-THETH
JETHRO	JETH'-RO
JETUR	JEE'-TUR
JEUEL	JOO'-EL
JEUSH	JEE'-OOSH
JEUZ	JEE'-UZZ
JEZANIAH	JEZ-AN-EYE'-YA
AZARIAH	AZ-AR-EYE'-YA
JEZEBEL	JEZ'-E-BELL
JEZER	JEE'-ZER
JEZERITES	JEE'-ZER-IGHTS
JEZIEL	JEZ-EYE'-EL
JEZRAHIAH	JEZ-RA-HIGH'-YA
JEZREEL	JEZ'-RE-EL
JEZREELITE	JEZ'-RE-EL-IGHT'
JEZREELITESS	JEZ'-RE-EL-IGHT'-ESS
JIDLAPH	JID'-LAFF
JOAB	JOH'-AB

JOACHAZ	JOH'-AKH-AZ
JEHOAHAZ	JE-HOH'-A-HAZ
JOAH	JOH'-A
	YOH'-A
JOAHAZ	JOH'-A-HAZ
JEHOAHAZ	JE-HOH'-A-HAZ
JOAKIM	JOH'-A-KIM
JOANAN	JOH'-A-NAN
JOANNA	JOH-AN'-NA
JOARIB	JOH'-A-RIB
JEHOIARIB	JE-HOI'-YA-RIB
JOASH	JOH'-ASH
JEHOASH	JE-HOH'-ASH
JOB	JOHB'
	E-YOHB'
JOBAB	JOH'-BAB
JOCHEBED	YOKH'-A-BED
JODA	JOH'-DA
JODAN	JOH'-DAN
JOED	JOH'-ED
	YOH'-ED
JOEL	JOH'-EL
	YOH'EL
JOELAH	JOH-EH'-LA
JOEZER	YOH-EEZ'-ER
JOGBEHAH	JOGG'-BE-HA
JOGLI	JOGG'-LIE
JOHA	JOH'-HA
JOHANAN	YOH'-HA-NAN
JOHN	JONN'
JOIADA	YOI'-A-DA
JEHOIADA	JE-HOI'-A-DA
JOIAKIM	YOI'-A-KIM
JOIARIB	YOI'-A-RIB
JEHOIARIB	JE-HOI'-A-RIB
JOKIM	YOH'-KIM
JOKMEAM	JOK'-ME-AM
JOKNEAM	JOK'-NE-AM
JOKSHAN	JOK'-SHAN
JOKTAN	JOK'-TAN
JOKTHEEL	JOK'THA-EL
JONADAB	JOH'-NA-DAB
JEHONADAB	JE-HOH'-NA-DAB
JONAH	JOH'-NA

JONAM	JOH'-NAM
JONATHAN	JONN'-A-THANN
	YOH'-NA-THAN
JOPPA	JOPP'-A
JORAH	JOHR'-A
JORAI	JOHR'-EYE
JORAM	JOH'-RAM
	YOH'-RAM
JEHORAM	JE-HOH'-RAM
	YEH-HOH'-RAM
JORDAN	JOR'-DAN
JORIM	JOHR'-IM
JORKEAM	JOR'-KE-AM
JOSECH	JOH'-SEKH
JOSEPH	JOH'-SEF
JOSES	JOH'-SES
JOSHAH	JOH'-SHA
JOSHAPHAT	JOSH'-A-FAT
JOSHAVIAH	JOSH-A-VYE'-A
JOSHBEKASHAH	JOSH-BE-KA'-SHA
JOSHEB-BASSHEBETH	JO'-SHIB-BA-SHE'-BETH
JOSHIBIAH	JOSH-IBB-EYE'YA
JOSHUA	JOSH'-OO-A
	YESH-OO'-A
JOSIAH	JOH-SIGH'-A
	JE-SIGH'-YA
JOSIPHIAH	JOSS-IF-EYE'-YA
JOTBAH	JOT'-BA
JOTBATHAH	JOT'-BA-THA
JOTHAM	JOH'-THAM
JOZABAD	JOH'-ZA-BAB
JOZACAR	JOH'-ZA-KHAR
JOZADEK	JOH'-ZA-DAK
JEHOZADEK	JE-HOH'-ZA-DEK
JUBAL	JOOB'-AL
JUCAL	JOO'-KHAL
JUDAH	JOO'-DA
JUDAISM	JOO'-DA-ISM
JUDAIZING	JOO'-DA-IZE-ING'
JUDAS	JOO'-DAS
JUDAS MACCABEUS	JOO'-DAS-MAK'-A-BE'-US
JUDE	JOOD'
JUDEA	JOOD-E'-A
JUDITH	JOOD'-ITH

JULIA	JOOL'-I-A
JULIUS	JOOL'-I-US
JUNIA	JOON'-I-A
JUSHAB-HESED	JOO'-SHIB-KHES'-ED
JUSTUS	JOOS'-TUS
JUTTAH	JUTT'-A

– K –

KABZEEL	KAB'-ZE-EL
JEKABZEEL	JE-KAB'-ZE-EL
KADESH	KEH'-DESH
KADESH-BARNEA	KEH'-DESH-BAR-NEE'-A
KADMIEL	KAD'-MI-EL
KAIN	KEHN'
KALLAI	KAL'-EYE
KAMON	KA'-MON
KANAH	KA'-NA
KAREAH	KA-REE'-A
KARKA	KAR'-KA
KARKOR	KAR'-KOHR
KARNAIM	KAR-NA'-IM
KARTAN	KAR'-TAN
KATTATH	KATT'-ATH
KEDAR	KEE'-DAR
KEDARITES	KEE'-DA-RIGHTS
KEDEMAH	KED'-E-MA
KEDEMOTH	KED'-E-MOTH
KEDESH	KEDD'-ESH
KEDRON	KEE'-DRON
KEHELATHAH	KE-HEH-LAH'-THA
KEILAH	KE-EYE'-LA
KELAIAH	KEL-A'-YAH
KELITA	KEL-EYE'-TA
KEMUEL	KE-MOO'-EL
KENAN	KEE'-NAN
CAINAN	KEH'-NAN
KENATH	KEN'-ATH
KENAZ	KEN'-AZ
KENIZZITE	KEN'-IZ-ZIGHTS
KENITES	KEN'-IGHTS
KEREN-HAPPUCH	KER'-EN-HAPP'-AKH
KERIOTH	KER'-I-OTH
KERIOTH-HEZRON	KER'-I-OTH-HEZ'-RON

KEROS	KER'-OS
KETAB	KEH'-TAB
KETURAH	KE-TOO'-RA
KEZIAH	KEZ-EYE'-A
KIBROTH-HATTAAVAH	KIB'-ROTH-HAT'-TA-VAH
KIBZAIM	KIB-ZA'-YIM
KIDRON	KID'-RON
KILAN	KY'-LAN
KINAH	KY'-NA
KIR	KIRR'
KIR-HARESETH	KIRR'-HARR'-E-SETH
KIR-HERES	KIRR-HERR'-ES
KIRIATH	KIRR'-I-ATH
KIRIATHAIM	KIRR'-I-ATH-A'-YIM
KIRIATH-ARBA	KIRR'-I-ATH-AR'-BA
HEBRON	HE'-BRON
KIRIATH-HUZOTH	KIRR'-I-ATH-HOO'-ZOTH
KIRIATH-JEARIM	KIRR'-I-ATH-JEE'-A-RIM
KIRIATH-ARIM	KIRR'-I-ATH-A'-RIM
KIRIATH-BAAL	KIRR'-I-ATH-BA'-AL
BAALAH	BA'-AL-A
BAALE JUDAH	BA'-AL-E-JOO'-DA
KIRIATH-SANNAH	KIRR'-I-ATH-SAN'-A
KIRIATH-SEPHER	KIRR'-I-ATH-SEH'-FER
KISH	KISH'
KISHI	KISH'-EYE
KUSHAIAH	KOO-SHA'-YA
KISHION	KISH'-I-ON
KISHON	KY'-SHON
KITRON	KIT'-RON
KITTIM	KITT'-IM
KOA	KOH'-A
KOHATH	KOH'-HATH
KOHATHITE	KOH'-HATH-IGHT
KOHELETH	KOH-HELL'-ETH
QOHELETH	KOH-HELL'-ETH
KOLA	KOH'-LA
KOLAIAH	KOH-LA'-YAH
KONA	KOH'-NA
KORAH	KOHR'-A
KORAHITES	KOHR'-A-IGHTS
KORE	KOH'-RE
KOZ	KOZZ'
KUE	KOO'-EYE

KUSHAIAH	KOO-SHA'-YA

– L –

LAADAH	LA'-A-DA
LABAN	LEH'-BAN
LACCUNUS	LA-KOO'-NUS
LACEDAEMONIANS	LASS'-E-DY-MOH'-NI-ANS
LACHISH	LAKH'-ISH
LADAN	LA'-DAN
LAEL	LA'-EL
LAHAD	LA'-HAD
LAHMAM	LA'-MAM
LAHMI	LA'-MY
LAISH	LA'-ISH
LAISHAH	LA'-ISH-A
LAKKUM	LAKK'-UM
LAMECH	LAM'-EKH
LAODICEA	LEH'-O-DI-SEE'-A
LAODICEANS	LEH'-O-DI-SEE'-ANS
LAPPIDOTH	LAP'-ID-OTH
LASEA	LAS-E'-A
LASHA	LA'-SHA
LASHARON	LA-SHAR'-ON
LASTHENES	LASTH'-E-NES
LATIN	LAT'-IN
LAZARUS	LAZ'-A-RUS
LEAH	LEE'-A
LEBANA	LE-BA'-NA
LEBANAH	LE-BA'-NA
LEBANON	LEB'-AN-ON
LEBAOTH	LEB'-A-OTH
LEBBEUS	LE-BE'-US
LEBONAH	LE-BOH'-NA
LECAH	LEH'-KHA
LEGION	LEEJ'-ON
LEHABIM	LE-HA'-BIM
LEHEM	LE'-HEM
LEHI	LE'-HIGH
LEMUEL	LEM'-OO-EL
LESHEM	LESH'-EM
LAISH	LA'-ISH
LETUSHIM	LE-TOOSH'-IM
LEUMMIM	LE-UMM'-IM

LEVI	LEE'-VI
LEVITES	LEE'-VIGHTS
LEVITICUS	LEV-IT'-I-KUS
LEVIATHAN	LE-VY'-ATH-AN
LIBNAH	LIB'-NA
LIBNI	LIB'-NYE
LIBNITES	LIB'-NIGHTS
LIBYA	LIB'-I-A
LIBYANS	LIB'-I-ANS
LIKHI	LIK'-HIGH
LINUS	LIE'-NUS
LOD	LOD'
LYDDA	LID'-DA
LO-DEBAR	LO-DE-BAR'
LOT	LOTT'
LOTAN	LO'-TAN
LOTHASUBUS	LOTH-A'-SUB-US
HASHUM	HASH'-UM
LOZON	LOH'-ZON
DARKON	DAR'-KON
LUBIM	LOO'-BIM
LUCIUS	LOO'-SHUSS
LUD	LUDD'
LUDIM	LOO'-DIM
LUHITH	LOO'-HITH
LUKE	LOOK'
LUZ	LUZZ'
LYCAONIA	LIKK-A-OH'-NI-A
LYCAONIAN	LIKK-A-OH'-NI-AN
LYCIA	LISH'-I-A
LYDIA	LIDD'-I-A
LYSANIAS	LI-SAN'-I-AS
LYSIAS	LISS'-I-AS
[CLAUDIUS] LYSIAS	[KLAW'-DI-US] LISS'-I-AS
LYSIMACHUS	LISS-IM'-AKH-US
LYSTRA	LISS'-TRA

— M —

MAACAH	MA'-AKH-A
MAACATHITE	MA-A'-KHA-THIGHT
MAACATH	MA-AK'-ATH
[ARAM]-MAACAH	[AR'-AM]-MA'-AKH-A
MAADAI	MA'-A-DYE
MAADIAH	MA-AD'-YAH

MAAI	MA'-EYE
[MAALEH]-ACRABBIM	[MA'-A-LE]-A-KRABB'-IM
AKRABBIM	A-KRABB'-IM
MAARATH	MA'-A-RATH
MAASAI	MA'-AS-EYE
MAASEIAH	MA-AS-EYE'-YAH
MASSEIAH	MASS-EYE'-YAH
MOOSSIAS	MOH-SIGH'-AS
MAASMAS	MA-AS'-MAS
MAATH	MA'-ATH
MAAZ	MA'-AZ
MAAZIAH	MA-A-ZYE'-YAH
MACCABEE	MAK'-A-BE
[JUDAS] MACCABEUS	[JOO'-DAS] MAK-A-BE'-US
MACEDONIA	MASS-ED-OH'-NI-A
MACEDONIAN	MASS-ED-OH'-NI-AN
MACHBANNAI	MAKH-BANN'-EYE
MACHBENA	MAKH-BE'-NA
MACHI	MAKH'-EYE
MACHIR	MAKH'-EER
MACHIRITES	MAKH'-IRR-IGHTS
MACHNADBEAI	MAKH-NAD'-BE-EYE
MACHPELAH	MAKH-PE'-LA
MACRON	MAK'-RON
MADAI	MA'-DIE
MADMANNAH	MADH-MAN'-A
MADMEN	MADH'-MEN
MADMENAH	MADH-MEN'-A
MADON	MA'-DONN
MAGADAN	MAG'-A-DAN
DALMANUTHA	DAL-MAN-OO'-THA
[MAGDALA]	[MAG'-DA-LA]
MAGDALENE	MAG'-DA-LEEN
MAGDIEL	MAG'-DI-EL
[MAGI]	[MEH'-JY]
MAGOG	MAG'-OGG
MAGPIASH	MAG'-PI-ASH
MAHALAB	MA'-HA-LAB
AHLAB	AH'-LAB
MAHALALEL	MA-HA'-LA-LELL
MAHALALEEL	MA-HA'-LA-LEEL
MAHANAIM	MA-HA-NA'-IM
MAHANEH-DAN	MAH'-A-NE-DAN'
MAHARAI	MAH'-AR-EYE

63

MAHATH	MA'-HATH
MAHAVITE	MA'-HA-VIGHT
MAHLAH	MAH'-LA
MAHLI	MAH'-LIE
MAHLITE	MAH'-LIGHT
MAHLON	MAH'-LON
MAHOL	MA'-HOL
MAHSEIAH	MA-SE'-YAH
MAKAZ	MAH'-KAZ
MAKED	MA'-KED
MAKHELOTH	MAK'-EL-OTH
MAKKEDAH	MA-KEH'-DA
MALACHI	MAL'-AKH-EYE
MALCAM	MAL'-KHAM
MALCHIAH	MAL-KHY'-YAH
MALCHIJAH	MAL-KHY'-YAH
MELCHIAS	MEL'-KI-AS
MALCHIEL	MAL'-KI-EL
MALCHIELITE	MAL'-KI-EL-IGHT
MALCHIRAM	MAL-KHY'-RAM
MALCHISHUA	MAL'-KE-SHOO'-A
MALCHUS	MAL'-KHUS
MALLOTHI	MAL'-E-THIGH
MALLUCH	MAL'-UKH
MALLUCHI	MAL-OOKH'-EYE
MALLUS	MALL'-US
MALTA	MAHL'-TA
MAMDAI	MAM'-DIE
BENAIAH	BEN-EYE'-YAH
MAMRE	MAM'-RE
MANAEN	MAN'-A-EN
MANAHATH	MAN'-A-HATH
MANAHATHITES	MAN'-A-HATH'-IGHTS
MANASSEH	MAN-ASS'-E
MANASSITE	MAN-ASS'-IGHT
[TITUS] MANIUS	[TIE'-TUS] MAN'-I-US
MANOAH	MAN-OH'-A
MAOCH	MA'-OKH
MAON	MA'-ON
MAONITES	MA'-ON-IGHTS
MARA	MAR'-A
MARAH	MAR'-A
MARANATHA	MA'-RA-NA-THA'
MAREAL	MA'-RE-AL

MARESHAH	MA-REH'-SHA
MARISA	MA-RI'-SA
[JOHN] MARK	[JON] MARK'
MAROTH	MAH'-ROTH
MARSENA	MAR'-SE-NA
MARTHA	MAR'-THA
MARY	MEH'RE
MASH	MASH'
MASHAL	MA'-SHAL
MASIAH	MAS-EYE'-A
MASREKAH	MAS'-RE-KA
MASSA	MASS'-A
MASSAH	MASS'-A
MATRED	MAT'-RED
MATRITES	MAT'-RIGHTS
MATTANAH	MAT-TA'-NA
MATTANIAH	MAT-TAN-EYE'-YAH
MATTATHA	MAT'-A-THA
MATTATHIAS	MA-TA-THIGH'-AS
MATTATTAH	MAT'-A-TA
MATTENAI	MAT'-E-NIGH
MATTHAN	MATH'-AN
MATTHAT	MATH'-AT
MATTHEW	MATH'-EW
MATTHIAS	MATH-EYE'-AS
MATTITHIAH	MAT'-I-THIGH'-A
MATTATHIAH	MAT'-A-THIGH'-A
MAZZAROTH	MAZZ'-A-ROTH
MEARAH	ME-AR'-A
MEBUNNAI	ME-BUNN'-EYE
MECHERATHITE	MEKH-ER'-A-THIGHT
MECONAH	MEKH-OH'-NA
MEDAD	ME'-DAD
MEDAN	ME'-DAN
MEDEBA	ME'-DE-BA
MEDIA	MEED'-I-A
MEDES	MEEDS'
MEGIDDO	ME-GIDD'-O
ARMAGEDDON	AR-MA-GEDD'-ON
MEHETABEL	ME-HET'-A-BEL
MEHIDA	ME-HIGH'-DA
MEHOLATHITE	ME-HO'-LA-THIGHT
MEHUJAEL	ME-HOO'-JA-EL

ME-JARKON	ME-JAR'-KONN
MELATTIAH	MEL'-A-TIE'-YAH
MELCHI	MEL'-KHI
MELCHIEL	MEL'-KHI-EL
MELCHIZEDEK	MEL-KHIZ'-ED-EK
MELEA	MEL'-E-A
MELECH	MEL'-EKH
[QUINTUS] MEMMIUS	[KWIN'-TUS] MEM'-MI-US
MEMPHIS	MEM'-FIS
MEMUCAN	MEM-OOKH'-AN
MENAHEM	MEN'-A-HEM
MENE, MENE, TEKEL, & PARSIN	MEN'-E, MEN'-E, TEK'-EL, and PAR'-SIN
MENE, MENE, TEKEL, UPHARSIN	MEN'-E, MEN'-E, TEK'-EL, YOU-FAR'-SIN
MENELAUS	MEN-E-LEH'-US
MENESTHEUS	MEN-ESTH'-E-US
MENI	MEN'-E
MENNA	MEN'-NA
MENUHOTH	MEN-OO'-THOTH
MEONOTHAI	ME-OH'-NOTH-EYE
MEPHAATH	MEF-A'-ATH
MEPHIBOSHETH	MEF-IB'-OSH-ETH
MERIBAAL	MER'-I-BA-AL
MERAB	MEH'-RAB
MERAIAH	ME-RA'-YAH
MERAIOTH	ME-RA'-YOTH
MERARI	ME-RA'-RYE
MERARITES	ME-RA'-RIGHTS
MERATHAIM	MER-A-THAH'-IM
MERED	MER'-ED
MEREMOTH	MER'-E-MOTH
MERES	MER'-ES
MERIBAH	MER'-I-BA
MERIBATH-KADESH	MER'-I-BATH-KEH'-DESH
KADESH-BARNEA	KEH'-DESH-BAR-NEE'-A
MERIBAAL	MER'-I-BA'-AL
MERIBBAAL	MER'-IB-BA'-AL
MEPHIBOSHETH	MEF'-I-BOSH'-ETH
MERODACH	ME-ROH'-DAKH
[MARDUK]	[MAR'-DOOK]
MERODACH-BALADAN	ME-ROH'-DAKH-BAL'-A-DAN
MEROM	MER'-OHM
MERONOTHITE	ME-RON'-O-THIGHT

MEROZ	MER'-OZ
MERRAN	MER'-AN
MIDIAN	MID'-I-AN
MESALOTH	MES'-A-LOTH
MESHA	MEE'-SHA
	MEH'-SHA
MESHACH	MEE'-SHAKH
MESHECH	MESH'-EKH
MESHELEMIAH	ME-SHELL'-EM-EYE'-A
MESHEZABEL	ME-SHEZ'-A-BEL
MESHILLEMOTH	ME-SHILL'-EM-OTH
MESHILLEMITH	ME-SHILL'-EM-ITH
MESHOBAB	ME-SHOH'-BAB
MESHULLAM	ME-SHOOL'-AM
MESHULLEMETH	ME-SHOOL'-EM-ETH
METHEG-AMMAH	METH'-EG-AM'-MA
METHUSELAH	METH-OO'-ZEL-A
METHUSHAEL	METH-OO'-SHA-EL
MEUNIM	ME-OO'-NIM
MEUNITES	ME-OO'-NIGHTS
MEZAHAB	MEZ'-A-HAB
MEZOBAITE	MEZ-OH'-BA-IGHT
MIBHAR	MIB'-HAR
MIBSAM	MIB'-SAM
MIBZAR	MIB'-ZAR
MICA	MY'-KA
MICAH	MY'-KA
MICAIAH	MIKH-EYE'-A
MICHAEL	MY'-KELL
MICHAL	MEE'-KHAL
MICHMASH	MIKH'-MASH
MICHMAS	MIKH'-MAS
MICHMETHATH	MIKH'-METH-ATH
MICHRI	MKH'-RYE
MIDDEN	MI'-DEEN
MIDIAN	MID'-I-AN
MIDIANITE	MID'-I-AN-IGHT
MIGDAL-EL	MIG'-DAL-EL
MIGDOL	MIG'-DOLL
MIGRON	MIG'-RON
MIJAMIN	MI-YAM'-IN
MIKLOTH	MIK'-LOTH
MIKNEIAH	MIK-NE'-YAH
MILALAI	MIL'-A-LYE

MILCAH	MIL'-KHA
MILCOM	MIL'-KHOHM
MILETUS	MY-LEE'-TUS
MILLO	MILL'-O
MINEANS	MI-NEE'-ANS
MINNI	MIN'-EYE
MINNITH	MINN'-ITH
MIRIAM	MIR'-I-AM
MIRMAH	MIR'-MA
MISHAEL	MISH'-A-EL
MISHAL	MISH'-AL
MISHAM	MISH'-AM
MISHMA	MISH'-MA
MISHMANNAH	MISH-MAN'-A
MISHRAITES	MISH'-RA-IGHTS
MISPAR	MIS'-PAR
MISREPHOTH-MAIM	MIS'-RE-FOTH-MA'-IM
MITHKATH	MITH'-KATH
MITHNITE	MITH'-NIGHT
MITHREDATH	MITH'-RE-DATH
MITHRIDATES	MITH'-RE-DA'-TES
MITYLENE	MIT'-EL-EE'-NE
MIZAR	MIZ'-AR
MIZPAH	MIZ'-PA
MIZPEH	MIZ'-PE
MIZRAIM	MIZ'-RA-IM
MIZZAH	MIZZ'-A
MNASON	NEH'-SON
MOAB	MOH'-AB
MOADIAH	MO-AD-EYE'-A
MOCHMUR	MOKH'-MUR
MODEIN	MOD'-EN
MOETH	MO'-ETH
MOLADAH	MOL'-A-DA
MOLECH	MOH'-LEKH
MOLOCH	MOH'-LOKH
MOLID	MOH'-LID
MOOSSIAS	MOO'-SI-AS
MAASEIAH	MA-AS-EYE'-A
MORDECAI	MOR'-DEK-EYE
MOREH	MOHR'-E
MORESHETH	MOHR'-ESH-ETH
MORIAH	MOH-RYE'-A

MOSERAH	MOH-SER'-A
MOSEROTH	MOH-SER'-OTH
MOSES	MOH'-ZIZ
MOZA	MOH'-ZA
MOZAH	MOH'-ZA
MUPPIM	MUPP'-IMM
MUSHI	MOO'-SHY
MUSHITES	MOO'-SHIGHTS
MYNDOS	MIN'-DOS
MYRA	MY'-RA
MYSIA	MISS'-I-A

– N –

NAAM	NA'-AM
NAAMAH	NA'-A-MA
NAAMAN	NEH'-A-MAN
	NA'-AM-AN
NAAMITE	NA'-AM-IGHT
NAAMATHITE	NA'-AM-ATH-IGHT
NAARAH	NA'-AR-A
NAARAN	NA'-AR-AN
NAARAI	NA'-AR-EYE
NAATHUS	NA'-ATH-US
NABAL	NEH'-BAL
	NAH'-BAL
NABARIAH	NA'-BAR-EYE'-A
NABATEANS	NA-BA-TEE'-ANS
NABOTH	NEH'-BOTTH
	NAH'-BOTTH
NACON	NAKH'-ON
NADAB	NA'-DAB
NADABATH	NAD'-A-BATH
NAGGAI	NAG'-EYE
NAHALAL	NA'-HA-LAL
NAHALOL	NA'-HA-LOLL
NAHALIEL	NA-HAL'-I-EL
NAHAM	NA'-HAM
NAHAMANI	NA-HA-MAHN'E
NAHARI	NA'-HAR-EYE
NAHASH	NA'-HASH
NAHATH	NA'-HATH
NAHBI	NA'-BE
NAHOR	NA'-HOR
NAHSHON	NA'-SHON

NAHUM	NEH'-HUM
	NA'-HUM
NAIN	NEHN'
NAIOTH	NYE'-OTH
NANEA	NAN-E'-A
NAOMI	NEH-OH'-ME
	NA'-O-ME
NAPHATH	NAF'-ATH
NAPHATH-DOR	NA'-FATH-DOR
NAPHOTH-DOR	NA'-FOTH-DOR
NAPHISH	NAF'-ISH
NAPHTALI	NAF'-TA-LIE
NAPHTUHIM	NAF'-TO-HIM
NATHAN	NEH'-THANN
NATHANAEL	NATH-AN'-E-EL
NATHAN-MELECH	NEH'-THANN-MEL'-EKH
NAZARENE	NAZ'-AR-EEN
NAZARETH	NAZ'-AR-ETH
NAZARITE	NAZ'-AR-IGHT
NEAH	NEH'-A
NEAPOLIS	NE-AP'-OLL-ISS
NEARIAH	NE-AR-EYE'-A
NEBAI	NE'-BY
NEBAIOTH	NE-BYE'-OTH
NEBALLAT	NE-BAL'-AT
NEBAT	NE'-BAT
NEBO	NEE'-BO
NEBUCHADNEZZAR	NEB'-UKH-AD-NEZZ'-AR
NEBUCHADREZZAR	NEB'-UKH-AD-RED'-ZAR
NEBUSHAZBAN	NEB'-USH-AZ'-BAN
NEBUZARADAN	NEB'-UZ-A-RAH'-DAN
NECO	NEKH'-O
NEDABIAH	NED'-A-BYE'-AH
NEHELAM	NE-HELL'-AM
NEHEMIAH	NE-HEM-EYE'-A
NEHUM	NE'-HUM
NEHUSHTA	NE-HOOSH'-TA
NEIEL	NE-EYE'-EL
NEKODA	NE-KOH'-DA
NEMUEL	NEM'-OO-EL
NEMUELITE	NEM'-OO-EL-IGHTS
NEPHEG	NEF'-EGG
NEPHILIM	NEF'-ILL-IM

NEPHISIM	NEF'-IS-IM
NEPHUSHESIM	NEF-OOSH'-ES-IM
NEPHTOAH	NEF-TOH'-A
NER	NER'
NERAIAH	NER-EYE'-A
NERIAH	NER-EYE'-A
NEREUS	NEE'-RE-US
NERGAL	NER'-GAL
NERGAL-SHAREZER	NER'-GAL-SHA-REZ'-AR
NERI	NER'-I
NERIAH	NER-EYE'-A
NERAIAH	NER-EYE'-A
NETAIM	NE-TA'-IM
NETHANEL	NETH'-AN-EL
NETHANIAH	NETH-AN-EYE'-A
NETHINIM	NETH'-IN-IM
NETOPHAH	NE-TOH'-FA
NETOPHAHTITES	NE-TOH'-FATH-IGHTS
NEZIAH	NEZ-EYE'-A
NEZIB	NEZ'-IB
NIBHAZ	NIB'-HAZ
NIBSHAN	NIB'-SHAN
NICANOR	NICK-EH'-NOR
	NICK-A'-NOR
NICODEMUS	NICK-O-DEE'-MUS
NICOLAITANS	NICK-O-LA'-IT-ANS
NICOLAUS	NICK'-O-LASS
NICOPOLIS	NICK-OP'-OL-IS
NIGER	NI'-GER
NILE	NYLE'
NIMRAH	NIM'-RA
NIMROD	NIM'-ROD
NIMSHI	NIM'-SHY
NINEVEH	NIN'-E-VE
NISROCH	NIS'-ROKH
NOADIAH	NOH'-AD-EYE'-A
NOAH	NOH'-A
NOB	NOBB'
NOBAH	NOH'-BA
NOD	NOD'
NODAB	NOH'-DAB
NOGAH	NOH'-GA
NOHAH	NOH'-HA

NUMENIUS	NOO-MEH'-NI-US
NUN	NOON'
NYMPHA	NIM'-FA

– O –

OBADIAH	OH-BA-DYE'-A
OBAL	OH'-BAL
EBAL	EE'-BAL
OBED	OH'-BED
OBED-EDOM	OH'-BED-EED'-OM
OBIL	OH'-BIL
OBOTH	OHB'-OTH
OCHIEL	OKH'-I-El
JEIL	JY'-EL
OCINA	OK-EYE'-NA
ODED	OH'-DED
ODOMERA	OD'-OM-E'-RA
OG	OGG'
OHAD	OH'-HAD
OHEL	OH'-EL
OHOLAH	O-HOH'-LA
OHOLIAB	O-HOH'-LI-AB
OHOLIBAH	O-HOH'-LI-BA
[MOUNT OF] OLIVES	OL'-IVES
OLIVET	OL'-IV-ET
OLYMPAS	OL-IM'-PAS
OLYMPIAN ZEUS	OL-IMP'-I-AN-ZEWS'
OMAR	OH'-MAR
OMEGA	OH-MEG'-A
	OH'-MEG-A
OMRI	OMM'-RI
ON	ONN'
ONAM	OH'-NAM
ONAN	OH'-NAN
ONESIMUS	O-NES'-I-MUS
	O-NEES'-I-MUS
ONESIPHORUS	ON-ES-IF'-OR-US
ONIAS	OH'-NY-AS
ONO	OHN'-OH
OPHEL	OH'-FEL
OPHIR	OH'-FIR
OPHNI	OFF'-NYE
OPHRAH	OFF'-RA

OREB	OH'-REB
OREN	OH'-REN
ORION	OR-EYE'-ON
ORPAH	OR'-PA
ORTHOSIA	OR-THOH'-SI-A
OSNAPPER	OS-NAP'-ER
OTHNI	OTH'-NYE
OTHNIEL	OTH'-NI-EL
OTHONIAH	OTH'-O-NYE'-A
OZEM	OHZ'-EM
OZIEL	OH'-ZI-EL
OZNI	OZ'-NYE
OZNITES	OZ'-NIGHTS

– P –

PAARAI	PA'-A-RYE
PADDAN	PAD'-AN
PADDAN-ARAM	PAD'-AN-AR'-AM
PAGIEL	PAG'-I-EL
PAHATH-MOAD	PAH'-HATH-MOH'-AB
PAI	PA'-EYE
PALAL	PAH'-LAL
PALESTINE	PAL'-ES-TYN
PALLU	PAL'-OO
PALLUITES	PAL'-OO-IGHTS
PALTI	PALT'-EYE
PALTIEL	PALT'-I-EL
PALTITE	PAL'-TIGHT
PAMPHYLIA	PAM-FILL'-I-A
PAPHOS	PA'-FOSS
PAPYRUS	PAP-EYE'-RUSS
PARAH	PAH'-RA
PARAN	PAH'-RAN
PARBAR	PAR'-BAR
PARMASHTA	PAR-MASH'-TA
PARMENAS	PAR'-MEN-AS
PARNACH	PAR'-NAK
PAROSH	PAR'-OSH
PARSHANDATHA	PAR'-SHAN-DAH'-THA
PARTHIANS	PARTH'-I-ANS
PARUAH	PAR-OO'-A
PARVAIM	PAR-VAH'-IM
PASAK	PA'-SAK

PAS-DAMMIN	PAS-DAM'-IM
PASEAH	PA-SEH'-A
PASHHUR	PASH'-OOR
PATARA	PA'-TA-RA
PATHROS	PATH'-ROS
PATMOS	PAT'-MOS
PATROBAS	PAT'-RO-BAS
PATROCLUS	PAT-ROCK'-LUS
PAU	PAH'-OO
PAI	PAH'-EYE
PAUL'	PAWL'
SAUL	SAWL'
[SERGIUS] PAULUS	[SER-JE-US] PAWL'-US
PEDAHEL	PED'-E-HEL
PEDAHZUR	PED-AH'-ZUR
PEDAIAH	PED-A'-YAH
PEKAH	PEK'-A
PEKAHIAH	PEK-A'-YAH
PEKOD	PEK'-OD
PELAIAH	PEL-A'-YAH
PELATIAH	PEL-A-TIE-YAH
PELEG	PEL'-EGG
PELET	PEL'-ET
PELETH	PEL'-ETH
PELETHITES	PEL'-ETH-IGHTS
PENIEL	PEN'-I-EL
PENUEL	PEN-OO'-EL
PENNINAH	PEN-IN'-A
PENTATEUCH	PEN'-TA-TEUKH
PENTECOST	PEN'-TE-KOST
PENUEL	PEN-OO'-EL
PENIEL	PEN'-I-EL
PEOR	PE'-OHR
PERAZIM	PER'-AZ-IM
PEREA	PER-EE'-A
PERESH	PER'-ESH
PEREZ	PER'-EZ
PEREZITES	PER'-EZ-IGHTS
PEREZ-UZZAH	PER'-EZ-UZ'-ZA
PEREZ-UZZA	PER'-EZ-UZ'-ZA
PERGA	PER'-GA
PERGAMUM	PER'-GA-MUM
PERIDA	PER-EYE'-DA
PERIZZITE	PER'-IZ-IGHT

PERSEPOLIS	PER-SEP'-O-LIS
PERSIA	PER'-ZHA
PERSIANS	PER'-ZHANS
PERSIS	PER'-SIS
PERUDA	PER-OO'-DA
PERIDA	PER-EYE'-DA
PETER	PEET'-ER
PETHAHIAH	PETH-A-HIGH'-YAH
PETHOR	PETH'-OHR
PETHUEL	PETH-OO'-EL
PEULLETHAI	PE-ULL'-ETH-EYE
PHANUEL	FAN-OO'-EL
PHARAKIM	FAR'-A-KIM
PHARAOAH	FEH'-RO
PHARAOH-HOPHRA	FEH'-RO-HOFF'-RA
PHARAOH-NECHO	FEH'-RO-NEKH'-O
PHARISEES	FARR'-ISS-EES
PHARPAR	FAR'-PAR
PHASELIS	FASS-EE'-LISS
PHASIRON	FASS-IR'-ON
PHICOL	FY'-KHOL
PHILADELPHIA	FILL-A-DELF'-I-A
PHILEMON	FY-LEE'-MON
PHILETUS	FY-LEE'-TUS
PHILIP	FILL'-IPP
PHILIPPI	FILL'-IPP-EYE
PHILIPPIANS	FILL-IPP'-I-ANS
PHILTSTIA	FILL-ISS'-TI-A
PHILISTINES	FILL'-ISS-TIGNS
PHILOLOGUS	FILL-O-LOG'-US
PHILOMETOR	FILL-O-MEE'-TOR
PHILOSOPHY	FILL-OSS'-OFF-E
PHINEAS	FINN'-E-AS
PHLEGON	FLEG'-ON
PHOEBE	FEE'-BE
PHOENICIA	FE-NISH'-A
PHOENICIANS	FE-NISH'-ANS
PHOENIX	FEE'-NIX
PHRYGIA	FRIDG'-I-A
PHYGELUS	FIDG'-EL-US
PHYLACTERIES	FY-LAC'-TER-I-ES
PI-BESETH	PIE'-BE-SETH
PI-HAHIROTH	PIE'-HA-HIGH'-ROTH
HAHIROTH	HA-HIGH'-ROTH

[PONTIUS] PILATE	[PON'-SHUS] PIE'-LAT
PILDASH	PILL'-DASH
PILHA	PILL'-HA
PILTAI	PILL'-TIE
PINON	PIE'-NON
PIRAM	PIE'-RAM
PIRATHON	PIRR'-A-THON
PIRATHONITE	PIRR'-A-THON-IGHT
PHARATHON	FAR'-A-THON
[MOUNT] PISGAH	[MOUNT] PIZ'-GA
PISHON	PIE'-SHON
PISIDIA	PI-SID'-I-A
PISPA	PISP'-A
PITHOM	PIE'-THOMM
PITHON	PIE'-THON
PLEIADES	PLY'-A-DEEZ
POCHERETH-HAZZEBAIM	POKH'-ER-ETH-HAZ-A-BA'-IM
PONTUS	PON'-TUS
PORATHA	POH-RA'-THA
POSIDONIUS	POSS-ID-OHN'-I-US
POTIPHAR	POT'-IF-AR
POTIPHERA	POT-IF'-E-RA
PRAETORIUM	PRY-TOHR'-I-UM
PRISCA	PRISS'-CA
PRISCILLA	PRISS-ILL'-A
PROCHORUS	PROKH'-OR-US
PROCONSUL	PRO-CONN'-SUL
PROCURATOR	PROK'-CURE-EH-TOR
PTOLEMAIS	TOL-E-MEH'-ISS
ACCO	AK'-KO
PTOLEMY	TOL'-E-ME
PUAH	POO'-A
PUBLIUS	POOB'-LI-US
PUDENS	POO'-DENS
PUL	POOL'
TIGLATH-PILESER	TIG'-LATH-PY-LEE'-SER
PUNITES	POO'-NIGHTS
PUNON	POO'-NON
PURAH	POO'-RA
PUR	POOR'
PURIM	POOR'-IM
PUT	POOT'
PUTEOLI	POO-TEE'-O-LI

PUTHITES	POO'-THIGHTS
PUTIEL	POO'-TI-EL
PUVAH	POO'-VA
PUAH	POO'-A
PYRRHUS	PIRR'-US

QOHELETH	KO-HELL'-ETH
KOHELETH	KO-HELL'-ETH
ECCLESIASTES	EK-KLES-I-ASS'-TEES
QUARTUS	KWAR'-TUS
QUINTUS MEMMIUS	KWIN'-TUS-MEMM'-I-US
QUIRINIUS	KWI-RIN'-I-US

RAAMAH	RA'-A-MA
RAAMA	RA'-A-MA
RAAMIAH	RA'-A-MY'-A
REELAIAH	RE'-EL-EYE'-A
RAAMSES	RA-AM'SES
RAMESES	RAM'-ES-ES
RABBAH	RAB'-BA
PHILADELPHIA	FILL-A-DELF'-I-A
AMMAN	A-MAHN'
RABBI	RABB'-EYE
RABBONI	RABB-OH'-NI
RABBITH	RABB'-ITH
RAB-MAG	RAB'-MAG
RAB-SARIS	RAB'-SA-RISS
RAB-SHAKEH	RAB'-SHA-KE
RACA	RA'-KA
RACAL	RAKH'-AL
RACHEL	REH'-TCHEL
	RAKH'-EHL
RADDAI	RAD'-EYE
RAGAE	RA'-GEH
REU	ROO'
RAGES	RA'-GESS
RAGUEL	RA-GOO'-EL
RAHAB	REH'-HAB
	RA'-HAB
RAHAM	RA'-HAM
RAKEM	RA'-KEM
RAKKATH	RAKK'-ATH

RAM	RAM'
RAMAH	RAH'-MAH
RAMATHAIM-ZOPHIM	RA'-MA-THA'-IM-ZOH'-FIM
RAMATHITE	RA'-MATH-IGHT
RAMATH-LEHI	RA'-MATH-LE'-HIGH
	RA'-MATH-LEE'-HY
RAMATH-MIZPEH	RA'-MATH-MIZ'-PE
RAMESES	RAM'-ES-ES
RAAMSES	RA-AM'-SES
RAMIAH	RA-MY'-A
RAMOTH	RA'-MOTH
JARMUTH	JAR'-MUTH
RAMOTH-GILEAD	REH'-MOTH-GIL'-E-AD
	RA'-MOTH-GIL'-E-AD
RAPHA	RA'-FA
RAPHAEL	RAF'-I-EL
	REH'-FI-EL
RAPHAH	RA'-FA
REPHAIAH	RE-FY'-A
RAPHAIM	RAF'-A-IM
RAPHIA	RAF-EYE'-A
RAPHON	RAF'-ON
RAPHU	RA'-FOO
RASSIS	RASS'-ISS
RATHAMIN	RATH'-A-MINN
RAZIS	RATS'-ISS
REAIAH	RE-EYE'-A
REBEKAH	RE-BEKK'-A
REBECCA	RE-BEKK'-A
RECAH	REH'-KA
RECHAB	REKH'-AB
RECHABITES	REKH'-A-BIGHTS
REELAIAH	RE-E-LIE'-YA
RAAMIAH	RA-A-MY'-A
RESAIAH	RE-SIGH'-YA
REGEM	REG'-EM
REGEM-MELECH	REG'-EM-MEL'-EKH
REHABIAH	RE-HA-BY'-AH
REHOB	RE'-HOHB
REHOBOAM	RE-HOHB-OH'-AM
REHOBOTH	RE-HOHB'-OTH
REHOBOTH-IR	RE-HOHB'-OTH-IRR
REHUM	RE'-HOOM
REI	REH'-EYE

REKEM	RECK'-EM
REMALIAH	RE-MA-LIE'-YA
REMETH	RE'-METH
REPHAH	RE'-FAH
REPHAIM	REF-AH'-IM
REPHAN	REF'-AN
REPHIDIM	REF'-I-DIM
RESAIAH	RES-EYE'-A
REELAIAH	REH-EL-EYE'-A
RESEN	RES'-EN
RESHEPH	RES'-EFF
REU	ROO'
REUBEN	ROO'-BEN
REUBENITE	ROO'-BEN-IGHT
REUEL	ROO'-EL
REUMAH	ROO'-MA
REZEPH	REZ'-EFF
REZIN	REZ'-IN
REZON	REZ'-ON
RHEGIUM	RHEJ'-I-UM
RHESA	RHE'-SA
RHODA	ROH'-DA
RHODES	ROHDS'
RHODOCUS	RODD'-O-KUSS
RIBAI	RY'-BY
RIBLAH	RIB'-LA
RIMMON	RIMM'-ON
RIMMONO	RIMM'-ON-O
RIMMON-PEREZ	RIMM'-ON-PER'-EZ
RINNAH	RINN'-A
RIPHATH	RY'-FATH
RISSAH	RISS'-A
RITHMAH	RITH'-MA
RIZIA	RIZ-EYE'-A
RIZPAH	RIZ'-PA
RODANIM	ROH'-DA-NIMM
ROGELIM	ROH'-GEL-IM
ROHGAH	ROH'-GA
ROMAMTI-EZER	ROH-MAM'-TIE-EZ'-ER
ROMANS	ROHM'-ANS
ROSH	ROHSH'
RUFUS	ROO'-FUS
RUMAH	ROO'-MA

– S –

SABACHTHANI	SA-BAKH-THAH'-NI
SABBAIAS	SABB'-I-AS
SHEMAIAH	SHE-MY'-AH
SABEANS	SA-BE'-ANS
SEBA	SE'-BA
SHEBA	SHE'-BA
SABTAH	SAB'-TA
SABTA	SAB'-TA
SABTECA	SAB-TEKH'-A
SACHAR	SAKH'-AR
SACHIA	SAKH-EYE'-A
SADDUCEES	SAD'-YOU-SEES
SAKKUTH	SAKK'-UTH
SALAMIS	SAL'-A-MISS
SALECAH	SAL'-EKH-A
SALEM	SAY'-LEM
SALIM	SAL'-IM
SALLAI	SALL'-EYE
SALLU	SALL'-OO
SALMA	SAL'-MA
SALMON	SAL'-MON
SALMONE	SAL-MOH'-NE
SALOME	SAL-OH'-ME
SAMARIA	SA-MEH'-RI-A
SAMARITANS	SAM-AR'-IT-ANS
SAMGAR-NEBO	SAM'-GAR-NEE'-BO
SAMLAH	SAM'-LA
SAMOS	SAY'-MOSS
SAMOTHRACE	SAM'-OTH-RACE
SAMPSAMES	SAMP'-SA-MES
SAMSON	SAM'-SON
SANBALLAT	SAN-BAL'-AT
SANHEDRIN	SAN'-ED-RINN
	SAN-HE'-DRINN
SANSANNAH	SAN-SAN'-A
SAPH	SAF'
SAPPHIRA	SAF-EYE'-RA
SARAH	SEH'-RA
SARAPH	SAR'-AFF
SARDIS	SAR'-DISS

SARGON	SAR'-GON
SAREA	SAH'-RE-A
SARID	SAH'-RID
SAROTHIE	SA-ROHTH'-E
SARSECHIM	SAR'-SEKH-IMM
SATAN	SEH'-TAN
SATHRABUZANES	SATH'-RA-BUZZ-AN'-ES
SHETHARBOZENAI	SHE'-THAR-BOHZ'-EN-EYE
SATRAP	SAT'-RAP
SAUL	SAWL'
SAVIAS	SAV-EYE'-AS
SCEVA	SEE'-VA
SCYTHIANS	SITH'-I-ANS
SCYTHOPOLIS	SITH-OP'-OL-ISS
BETHSHAN	BETH-SHAN'
SEBA	SEE'-BA
SECACAH	SEKH-AKH'-A
SECU	SEKH'-OO
SECUNDUS	SEK-OON'-DUS
SEGUB	SEE'-GUB
SEIR	SEER'
	SE'-EER
SEIRAH	SE-EER'-A
SELA	SEE'-LA
SELAH	SEE'-LA
SELEMIA	SEL-EEM'-I-A
SELEUCUS	SE-LOOK'-US
SELEUCIA	SE-LEW'-SEE-A
SEMACHIAH	SEM'-AKH-EYE'-A
SEMEIN	SEM-EYE'-EN
SENAAH	SE-NAH'-A
HASSENAAH	HASS-E-NAH'-A
SENEH	SEN'-E
SENIR	SEN'-EER
SENNACHERIB	SEN-AKH'-ER-IBB
SEORIM	SE-OH'-RIM
SEPHAR	SEFF'-AR
SEPHARAD	SE-FAH'-RAD
SEPHARVAIM	SEFF-AR-VA'-IM
SEPHARVITES	SEFF'-AR-VIGHTS
SEPTUAGINT	SEPT-OO'-A-JINT
SERAH	SERR'-A
SERAIAH	SERR-EYE'-AH

SERAPHIM	SER'-A-FIMM
SERED	SERR'-ED
SEREDITES	SERR'-ED-IGHTS
SERGIUS PAULUS	SER'-JE-US PAWL'-US
SERON	SERR'-ON
SERUG	SERR'-UG
SESTHEL	SES'-THEL
BEZALEL	BEZ'-A-LELL
SETH	SETH'
SETHUR	SE'-THOOR
SHAALBIM	SHA-AL'-BIMM
SHAALBON	SHA-AL'-BONN
SHAALIM	SHA-AL'-IMM
SHAAPH	SHA'-AFF
SHAARAIM	SHA-A-RAH'-IMM
SHAASHGAZ	SHA-ASH'-GAZZ
SHABBETHAI	SHABB'-ETH-EYE
SHADDAY	SHADD'-EYE
SHADRACH	SHAD'-RAKH
SHAGEE	SHA'-GEH
SHAHARAIM	SHA'-HA-RA'-IM
SHAHAZUMAH	SHA'-HAZ-OO'-MA
SHALISHAH	SHA-LIE'-SHA
SHALLECHETH	SHALL'-EKH-ETH
SHALLUM	SHALL'-UM
SHALMAI	SHALL'-MY
SHAMLAI	SHAM'-LIE
SHALMAN	SHALL'-MAN
SHALMANESER	SHALL'-MAN-EEZ'-ER
SHAMA	SHAH'-MA
SHAMGAR	SHAM'-GAR
SHAMHUTH	SHAM'-HOOTH
SHAMIR	SHAH'-MEER
SHAMLAI	SHAM'-LIE
SHALMAI	SHALL'-MY
SHAMMA	SHAH'-MAH
SHAMMAH	SHAM'-A
SHIMEA	SHIM'-E-A
SHIMEAH	SHIM'-E-A
SHIMEI	SHIM'-EYE
SHAMMOTH	SHAMM'-OTH
SHAMHUTH	SHAMM'-UTH
SHAMMAI	SHAMM'-EYE
SHAMMUA	SHAMM-OO'-A

SHAMSHERAI	SHAM'-SHER-EYE
SHAPHAM	SHAFF'-AM
SHAPHAN	SHAFF'-AN
SHAPHAT	SHAFF'-AT
SHAPHIR	SHAFF'-IR
SHARAI	SHAR'-EYE
SHARAR	SHAR'-ARR
SHAREZER	SHAR-EE'-ZER
SHARON	SHEH'-RON
SHARONITE	SHEH'-RON-IGHT
SHARUHEN	SHAR-OO'-HEN
SHASHAI	SHASH'-EYE
SHASHAK	SHAH'-SHAK
SHAUL	SHAH'-OOL
SHAULITES	SHAH'-OO-LIGHTS
SHAVEH	SHAH'-VEH
SHAVEH-KIRIATHAIM	SHAH'-VEH-KIR-YATH-A'-IM
SHAVSHA	SHAV'-SHA
SEREIAH	SER-EYE'-A
SHEVA	SHEH'-VA
SHISHA	SHY'-SHA
SHEAL	SHEH'-AL
SHEALTIEL	SHEH-AL'-TI-EL
SHEARIAH	SHEH-AR-EYE'-A
SHEBA	SHE-BA'
SHEBA [QUEEN OF]	SHEE'-BA
SHEBANIAH	SHEB'-AN-EYE'-A
SHEBARIM	SHEB-AH'-RIM
SHEBER	SHEBB'-ER
SHEBNA	SHEB'-NA
SHEBNAH	SHEB'-NA
SHEBUEL	SHEB-OO'-EL
SHUBAEL	SHOOB'-A-EL
SHECANIAH	SHEKH-AN-EYE'-A
SHECHEM	SHEKH'-EM
SHECHEMITES	SHEKH'-EM-IGHTS
SHEDEUR	SHED-EH'-OOR
SHEERAH	SHE'-ER-A
SHEHARIAH	SHE'-HAR-EYE'-A
[SHEKINAH]	[SHEK-EYE'-NA]
SHELAH	SHEH'-LA
SHELANITES	SHEH'-LAN-IGHTS
SHELEMIAH	SHEL'-E-MY'-A
MESHELEMIAH	ME-SHEL'-E-MY'-A

83

SHELEPH	SHEL'-EFF
SHELESH	SHEL'-ESH
SHELOMI	SHEL-OH'-MY
SHELOMITH	SHEL-OH'-MITH
SHELOMOTH	SHEL-OH'-MOTH
SHELUMIEL	SHEL-OOM'-E-EL
SALAMIEL	SAL-AM'-E-EL
SHEMA	SHEM-AH'
SHEMAAH	SHEM-A'-A
SHEMAIAH	SHEM-A'-YA
SABBAIAS	SABB-EYE'-AS
SHEMARIAH	SHEM'-AR-EYE'-A
SHEMEBER	SHEM-EH'-BER
SHEMED	SHEM'-ED
SHEMER	SHEM'-ER
SHOMER	SHOW'-MER
SHEMIDA	SHEM-EYE'-DA
SHEMIDAITES	SHEM-EYE'-DA-IGHTS
SHEMIRAMOTH	SHEM-IRR'-A-MOTH
SHEMUEL	SHEM-OO'-EL
SAMUEL	SAM'-YU-EL
SHENAZZAR	SHEN-AZ'-AR
SHEPHAM	SHEFF'-AM
SHEPHATIAH	SHEFF-AT-EYE'-A
SHEPHER	SHEH'-FER
SHEPHO	SHEFF'-O
SHEPHI	SHEFF'-EYE
SHEPUPHAM	SHEFF-OO'-FAM
SHEPHUPHAN	SHEFF-OO'-FAN
SHUPPIM	SHUPP'-IM
SHUPHAMITES	SHOO'-FAM-IGHTS
SHEREBIAH	SHER-E-BY'-A
SHERESH	SHER'-ESH
SHESHAI	SHESH'-EYE
SHESHAN	SHESH'-AN
SHESHBAZZAR	SHESH-BAZZ'-AR
SHETH	SHETH'
SHETHAR	SHEH'-AR
SHETHAR-BOZENAI	SHEH'-THAR-BOZ'-A-NE
SATHRABUZANES	SATH'-RA-BUZ'-A-NES
SHEVA	SHEV'-A
SHIBAH	SHY'-BA
SHIBBOLETH	SHIBB'-OL-ETH
SHIHOR	SHY'-HOR

SHIHOR-LIBNATH	SHY'-HORR-LIBB'-NATH
SHIKKERON	SHIKK'-ER-ON
SHILHI	SHILL'-HIGH
SHILHIM	SHILL'-HIM
SHARUHEN	SHAR-OO'-HEN
SHAARAIM	SHA-A-RA'-IM
SHILOAH	SHY-LO'-A
SILOAM	SIGH-LO'-AM
SHILOH	SHY'-LO
SHILONITE	SHY'-LO-NIGHT
SHIMEA	SHIMM'-E-A
SHAMMAH	SHAMM'-A
SHIMEATH	SHIMM'-E-ATH
SHIMEATHITES	SHIMM'-E-ATH-IGHTS
SHIMEI	SHIMM'-E-EYE
SHIMEITES	SHIMM'-E-IGHTS
SHEMA	SHEMM'A
SHIMON	SHY'-MONN
SHIMRATH	SHIMM'-RATH
SHIMRI	SHIMM'-RYE
SHIMRITH	SHIMM'-RITH
SHOMER	SHOW'-MER
SHIMRON	SHIM'-RON
SHIMRONITES	SHIM'-RON-IGHTS
SHIMRON-MERON	SHIM'-RON-MERR'-ON
SHIMSHAI	SHIM'-SHY
SHINAB	SHY'-NAB
SHINAR	SHY'-NAR
[SUMER]	[SOO'-MER]
SHIPHI	SHY'-FY
SHIPHMITE	SHIFF'-MIGHT
SHIPHRAH	SHIFF'-RATH
SHIPHTAN	SHIFF'-TAN
SHISHA	SHY'-SHA
SHAVSHA	SHAV'-SHA
SHISHAK	SHY'-SHAK
SHITTIM	SHE-TEEM'
SHIZA	SHY'-ZA
SHOAH	SHOH'-A
SHOBAB	SHOH'-BAB
SHOBACH	SHOH'-BAKH
SHOPHACH	SHOH'-FAKH
SHOBAI	SHOH'-BY
SHOBAL	SHOH'-BAL

SHOBEK	SHOH'-BEK
SHOBI	SHOH'-BY
SHOHAM	SHOW'-HAM
SHOMER	SHOW'-MER
SHEMER	SHEH'-MER
SHIMRITH	SHIM'-RITH
SHOPHACH	SHOH'-FAKH
SHOBACK	SHOH'-BAKH
SHUA	SHOO'-A
SHUAH	SHOO'-A
SHUHITE	SHOO'-HIGHT
SHUAL	SHOO'-AL
SHUBAEL	SHOO'-BA-EL
SHEBUEL	SHEBB'-OO-EL
SHUHAH	SHOO'-HA
SHUHAM	SHOO'-HAM
SHUHAMITES	SHOO'-HAM-IGHTS
SHUHITE	SHOO'-HIGHT
SHUAH	SHOO'-A
SHULAMMITE	SHOO'-LA-MIGHT
SHUMATHITE	SHOO'-MA-THIGHT
SHUNEM	SHOO'-NEM
SHUNNAMITE	SHOO'-NA-MIGHT
SHUNI	SHOON'-EYE
SHUNITES	SHOON'-IGHTS
SHUPPIM	SHUPP'-IM
SHUR	SHOOR'
SHUTHELAH	SHOO'-THEL-A
SHUTHELAHITES	SHOO'-THEL-A-HIGHTS
SIA	SHY'-A
SIAHA	SIGH'-A-HA
SIBBECAI	SIBB-EKH'-EYE
SIBBOLETH	SIBB'-OL-ETH
SIBMAH	SIB'-MA
SEBAM	SEB'-AM
SIBRAIM	SIB'-RA-IM
SICYON	SICK'-E-ON
SIDDIM	SIDD'-IM
SIDE	SIDD'-E
SIDON	SIGH'-DON
SIHON	SIGH'-HON
SILAS	SIGH'-LASS
SILVANUS	SILL-VEH'-NUS
SILLA	SILL'-A

SILOAM	SIGH-LOH'-AM
SIMALCUE	SIMM-AL'-KU-E
IMALKUE	IMM-AL'-KU-E
SIMEON	SIMM'-E-ON
SIMON	SIGH'-MON
SIMON MACCABEUS	SIGH'-MON MAKK'-A-BE'-US
SIMON MAGUS	SIGH'-MON MEH'-GUS
SIMON PETER	SIGH'-MON PEE'-TER
SIN	SEEN'
SINAI	SIGH'-NIGH
SINIM	SIGH'-NIMM
SINITES	SIGH'-NIGHTS
SIPHMOTH	SIFF'-MOTH
SIPPAI	SIPP'-EYE
SAPH	SAFF'
SIRACH	SEE'-RAKH
SIRAH	SIGH'-RA
SIRION	SIRR'-I-ON
SISERA	SISS'-ER-A
SISINNES	SISS'-IN-ES
SISMAI	SISS'-MY
SHESHAN	SHE'-SHAN
SITHRI	SITH'-RY
SITNAH	SIT'-NA
SMYRNA	SMIRR'-NA
[IZMIR]	[IZ-MEER']
SO	SOH'
SOCO	SOH'-KHOH
SOCOH	SOH'-KHOH
SODI	SOH'-DYE
SODOM	SODD'-OM
SODOMITE	SODD'-OM-IGHT
SOLOMON	SOL'-OM-ON
SULEIMAN	SOO-LIE'-MAN
SOPATER	SOH'-PA-TER
SOPHERETH	SOH'-FER-ETH
HASSOPHERETH	HA-SOH'-FER-ETH
SOREK	SOH'-REK
SOSIPATER	SOH-SIPP'-A-TER
SOSTHENES	SOHS'-THENN-ES
SOSTRATUS	SOH'-STRATT-US
SOTAI	SOH'-TY
SPAIN	SPEHN'

SPARTA	SPAR'-TA
SPARTANS	SPAR'-TANS
STACHYS	STA-KHISS
STEPHANAS	STEFF'-AN-AS
STEPHEN	STEE'-FEN
SUAH	SOO'-A
SUBAS	SOO'-BAS
SUCATHITES	SOOKH'-A-THIGHTS
SUCCOTH	SUKK'-OTH
SUCCOTH-BENOTH	SUKK'-OTH-BE'-NOHTH
SUD	SOOD'
SUDIAS	SOO'-DE-AS
HODAVIAH	HO-DAV-EYE'-AH
SUKKIIM	SUKK'-I-IMM
SUPH	SOOF'
SUPHAH	SOOF'-A
SUR	SOOR'
SUSA	SOO'-SA
SUSANNA	SOO-ZANN'-A
SUSI	SOO'-SIGH
SYCHAR	SIGH'-KHAR
SYENE	SIGH-EE'-NE
[ASWAN]	[AS-WAN']
SYMEON	SIMM'-E-ON
SYNTYCHE	SIN'TIKH-E
SYRACUSE	SIRR'-A-KOOS
SYRIA	SIRR'-I-A
SYRIANS	SIRR'-I-ANS
SYROPHOENICIA	SIGH'-ROH-FENN-ISH'-I-A
SYROPHOENICIAN	SIGH'-ROH-FENN-ISH'-I-AN
SYRTIS	SIRR'-TISS

– T –

TAANACH	TA'-AN-AKH
TAANATH-SHILOH	TA'-AN-ATH-SHY'-LO
TABBAOTH	TABB-AH'-OTH
TABBATH	TABB'-ATH
TABEEL	TABB'-E-EL
TABERAH	TABB'-E-RA
TABITHA	TABB'-ITH-A
DORCAS	DOR'-KASS
TABOR	TEH'-BORR
	TA'-BOR

TABRIMMON	TABB-RIMM'-ON
TADMOR	TADD'-MOHR
TAMAR	TA'-MAR
PALMYRA	PAL-MY'-RA
[TUDMUR]	[TOOD'-MOOR]
TAHAN	TAH'-AN
TAHANITES	TAH'-HAN-IGHTS
TAHASH	TA'-HASH
TAHATH	TA'-HATH
TAHCHEMONITE	TAKH-EM'-ON-IGHT
HACHMONITE	HAKH'-MON-IGHT
TAHPANHES	TA-PAN'-HES
TEHAPHNEHES	TE-HAF'-NE-HES
TAHPENES	TA'-PEN-ES
TAHREA	TA'-RE-A
TAHTIM-HODSHI	TA'-TIM-HODD'-SHY
TALITHA CUMI	TAL'-ITH-A KOO'-ME
TALMAI	TAL'-MY
TALMON	TAL'-MON
TAMAR	TA'-MAR
TAMMUZ	TAM'-MUZZ
THAMMUZ	THAM'-UZZ
TANHUMETH	TAN-HOO'-METH
TANIS	TAN'-ISS
ZOAN	ZOH'-AN
TAPHATH	TA'-FATH
TAPPUAH	TAP-OO'-A
TARALAH	TAR'-A-LA
TAREA	TAR'-E-A
TAHREA	TAR'-E-A
TARSHISH	TAR'-SHISH
TARSUS	TAR'-SUSS
TARTAK	TAR'-TAK
TARTAN	TAR'-TAN
TATTENAI	TAT'-E-NY
TEBAH	TEH'-BA
TEBALIAH	TE-BA-LIE'-YA
TEHAPHNEHES	TE-HAF'-NE-HES
TAHPANHES	TA-PAN'-HES
TEHINNAH	TE-HINN'-A
TEKOA	TE-KOH'-A
TEKOITES	TE-KOH'-IGHTS
TEL-ABIB	TEL-A-BIBB'
[TEL-AVIV]	[TEL-A-VEEV']

TELAH	TELL'-A
TELAIM	TELL-A'-IMM
TELEM	TELL'-EM
TEL-ASSAR	TELL-ASS'-AR
TELEM	TELL'-EM
TEL-HARSHA	TELL-HAR'-SHA
THELERSAS	THEL-ER'-SAS
[TELL EL-AMARNA]	[TELL'-EL-AM-AR'-NA]
[AKHETATON]	[AKH'-ET-AH-TON]
TEL-MELAH	TEL-MEH'-LA
THERMELETH	THER-MEH'-LETH
TEMA	TEH'-MA
TEMAN	TEH'-MAN
TEMANITE	TEH'-MAN-IGHT
TEMAH	TEH'-MA
TEMENI	TEM'-EN-EYE
TEPHON	TEFF'-ON
TERAH	TERR'-A
TERAPHIM	TERR'-A-FIMM
TERESH	TERR'-ESH
TERTIUS	TERSH'-I-US
TERTULLUS	TER-TULL'-US
TETRARCH	TET'-RARKH
THADDEUS	THADD-I'-US
JUDAS	JOO'-DASS
THAMMUZ	THAMM'-UZ
THASSI	THASS'-EYE
THEBES	THEEBS'
THEBEZ	THEBB'-EZ
THEODOTUS	THI-OD'-OT-US
THEOPHILUS	THI-OFF'-ILL-US
THERAS	THEH'-RAS
AHAVA	A'-HA-VA
THESSALONICA	THESS'-AL-ON-EYE'-KA
[SALONIKA]	[SAL-ON'-I-KA]
	[SAL-ON-EYE'-KA]
THESSALONIANS	THESS'-AL-OH'-NI-ANS
THEUDAS	THEW'-DAS
THISBE	THISS'-BE
THOMAS	TOMM'-AS
DIDYMUS	DID'-I-MUSS
THRACE	THREHS'
THUMMIM	THUMM'-IMM
THYATIRA	THIGH-A-TY'-RA

TIBERIAS	TY-BEER'-I-AS
TIBERIUS	TY-BEER'-I-US
TIBHATH	TIBB'-HATH
TIDAL	TY'-DALL
TIGLATH-PILESER	TIG'-LATH-PY-LEE'-SER
TILGATH-PILNESER	TIL'-GATH-PILL-NEE'-SER
TIGRIS	TY'-GRISS
HIDDEKEL	HID'-E-KELL
TIKVAH	TIK'-VAH
TOKHATH	TOK'-HATH
TILON	TY'-LON
TIMAEUS	TY-ME'-US
TIMNA	TIM'-NA
TIMNATH	TIM'-NATH
TIMNITE	TIM'-NIGHT
TIMNATH-HERES	TIM'-NATH-HER'-EZ
TIMNATH-SERAH	TIM'-NATH-SER'-A
TIMON	TY'-MON
TIMOTHY	TIM'-OTH-Y
TIPHSAH	TIFF'-SA
TIRAS	TY'-RAS
TIRATHITES	TIRR'-A-THIGHTS
TIRHAKAH	TIR-HA'-KA
TIRHANAH	TIR-HA'-NA
TIRIA	TIRR'-I-A
TIRZAH	TIRZ'-A
TISHBE	TISH'-BE
TISHBITE	TISH'-BIGHT
TITIUS JUSTUS	TIT'-I-US JUST'-US
TITUS	TY'-TUS
TITUS MANIUS	TY'-TUS MAN'-I-US
TIZITE	TY'-ZIGHT
TOAH	TOH'-A
TOB	TOBB'
TOBADONIJAH	TOBB'-AD-ON-EYE'-A
TOBIAH	TOHB'-EYE-A
TOBIJAH	TOHB-EYE'-YAH
TOBIAS	TOHB-EYE'-AS
TOBIT	TOHB'-IT
TOCHEN	TOKH'-EN
TOGARMAH	TOH-GAR'-MA
TOHU	TOH'-HOO
TOI	TOH'-EYE
TOU	TOH'OO

TOKNATH	TOK'-NATH
TIKVAH	TIK'-VA
TOLA	TOH'-LA
TOLAITES	TOH'-LA-IGHTS
TOLAD	TOH'-LAD
ELTOLAD	EL-TOH'-LAD
TOPARCHY	TOP'-AR-KHE
TOPHEL	TOH'-FEL
TORAH	TOH'-RA
TOU	TOH'-OO
TOI	TOH'-EYE
TRACHONITIS	TRAKH-ON-EYE'-TISS
TRIPOLIS	TRIP'-O-LISS
TROGYLLIUM	TROH-GILL'-I-UM
TROPHIMUS	TROH'-FIMM-US
TRYPHAENA	TRY-FEE'-NA
TRYPHO	TRY'-FO
TRYPHOSA	TRY-FOH'-SA
TUBAL	TOO'-BAL
TUBAL-CAIN	TOO'-BAL-KEHN'
TYCHICUS	TIKH'-I-KUSS
TYRANNUS	TI-RAN'-US
TYRE	TYR'
TYRIANS	TIRR'-I-ANS
TYROPOEON	TY-ROH'-PE-ON

– U –

UCAL	OOK'-AL
UEL	OO'-EL
JOEL	JO'-EL
ULAI	OO'-LIE
ULAM	OO'-LAM
ULLA	ULL'-A
UMMAH	UMM'-A
UNNI	UNN'-EYE
UNNO	UNN'-O
UPHAZ	OO'-FAZ
UR	OOR'
URBANUS	URR-BEH'-NUS
URI	YOO'-RYE
URIAH	YOO'-RYE-A
URIEL	YOO'-RI-EL
URIM	OO'-RIM
UTHAI	OO'-THIGH

UZ	UZZ'
UZAI	OO'-ZIGH
UZAL	OO'-ZAL
UZZAH	UZZ'-A
UZZA	UZZ'-A
UZZEN-SHEERAH	UZZ'-EN-SHEH'-ER-A
UZZI	UZZ'-EYE
UZZIAH	UZZ-EYE'-A
UZZIEL	UZZ'-I-EL
AZAREL	AZ'-A-REL
UZZIELITES	UZZ'-I-EL-IGHTS

– V –

VAIZATHA	VIE'-ZE-THA
VANIAH	VAN-EYE'-A
VASHTI	VASH'-TI
VOPHSI	VOFF'-SIGH

– W –

WAHEB	WA'-HEBB

– X –

XERXES	ZERK'-ZEES
AHASUERUS	A-HAS'-YOO-EHR'-US

– Y –

YAHWEH	YAH'-WEH
YIRON	YIRE'-ON

– Z –

ZAANAN	ZA'-AN-AN
ZAANANNIM	ZA'-AN-AN'-NIM
ZAAVAN	ZA'-A-VAN
ZABAD	ZA'-BAD
ZABBAI	ZABB'-EYE
ZABDI	ZABB'-DY
ZIMRI	ZIMM'-RE
ZABDIEL	ZABB'-DI-EL
ZABUD	ZABB'-UD
ZACCAI	ZAKH'-EYE
ZACCHAEUS	ZAKH-E'-US
ZACCUR	ZAKH'-OOR

ZADOK	ZAD'-OKK
ZAIR	ZA'-EER
ZALAPH	ZA'-LAF
ZALMON	ZAL'-MON
ZALMONAH	ZAL-MOH'-NA
ZALMUNNA	ZAL-MUNN'-A
ZAMZUMMIM	ZAM-ZUMM'-IM
ZANOAH	ZAN-OH'-A
ZAPHENATH-PANEAH	ZAFF'-EN-ATH-PAN-EH'-A
ZAPHON	ZAFF'-ON
ZAREPHATH	ZAR'-EFF-ATH
ZARETHAN	ZAR'-ETH-AN
ZARIUS	ZAR'-I-US
ZATTU	ZAT'-OO
ZAZA	ZA'-ZA
ZEBADIAH	ZEB'-A-DY'-A
ZERAIAH	ZER-EYE'-A
ZEBAH	ZE'-BA
ZEBEDEE	ZEB'-E-DEE
ZEBIDAH	ZEB-EYE'-DA
ZEBOIIM	ZEB-OY'-IM
ZEBOIM	ZEB-OH'-IM
ZEBUL	ZE'-BUL
ZEBULUN	ZEBB'-YU-LUN
ZEBULUNITE	ZEBB'-YU-LUN-IGHT
ZECHARIAH	ZEKH-AR-EYE'-A
ZEDAD	ZE'-DAD
ZEDEKIAH	ZEDD'-EK-EYE'-A
ZEEB	ZE'-EB
ZELA	ZEH'-LA
ZELEK	ZELL'-EK
ZELOPHEHAD	ZELL-OFF'-E-HAD
ZELZAH	ZEL'-ZA
ZEMARAIM	ZEM'-AR-AH'-IM
ZEMER	ZEM'-ER
ZEMARITES	ZEM'-AR-IGHTS
ZEMIRAH	ZEM-EYE'-RA
ZENAN	ZE'-NAN
ZENAS	ZE'-NAS
ZEPHANIAH	ZEFF'-AN-EYE'-A
ZEPHATH	ZE'-FATH
ZEPHATHAH	ZEFF-AH'-THA

ZEPHI	ZEFF'-EYE
ZEPHO	ZEFF'-OH
ZEPHON	ZEFF'-ON
ZEPHONITES	ZEFF'-ON-IGHTS
ZER	ZEHR'
ZERAH	ZER'-A
ZERAHITES	ZER'-A-HIGHTS
ZOHAR	ZOH'-HAR
ZERAIAH	ZER-A-HY'-A
ZEBADIAH	ZEB-A-DY'-A
ZERDAIAH	ZER-DA'-YA
AZIZA	AZ-EYE'-ZA
ZEREDA	ZER-EH'-DA
ZERERAH	ZER-EH'-RA
ZERESH	ZER'-ESH
ZERETH	ZER'-ETH
ZERETH-SHAHAR	ZER'-ETH-SHA'-HAR
ZERI	ZER'-EYE
ZEROR	ZER'-OR
ZERUAH	ZER-OO'-A
ZERUBBABEL	ZER-UBB'-A-BELL
ZERUIAH	ZER-OO-EYE'-A
ZETHAM	ZEH'-THAM
ZETHAN	ZEH'-THAN
ZETHAR	ZEH'-THAR
ZIA	ZY'-A
ZIBA	ZY'-BA
ZIBEON	ZIBB'-E-ON
ZIBIA	ZIBB-EYE'-A
ZICHRI	ZIKH'-RY
ZIDDIM	ZIDD'-IM
ZIHA	ZY'-A
ZIKLAG	ZIK'-LAG
ZILLAH	ZILL'-A
ZILLETHAI	ZILL'-ETH-EYE
ZILPAH	ZILL'-PA
ZIMMAH	ZIMM'-A
ZIMRAN	ZIMM'-RAN
ZIMRI	ZIMM'-RE
ZINA	ZY'-NA
ZIZAH	ZY'-ZA
ZION	ZY'-ON
ZIOR	ZY'-OR

ZIPH	ZIFF'
ZIPHITE	ZIFF'-IGHT
ZIPHAH	ZIFF'-A
ZIPHION	ZIFF'-I-ON
ZIPHRON	ZIFF'-RON
ZIPPOR	ZIPP'-OR
ZIPPORAH	ZIPP'-OR-A
ZIZ	ZIZZ'
ZIZA	ZY'-ZA
ZIZAH	ZY'-ZA
ZINA	ZY'-NA
ZOAN	ZOH'-AN
TANIS	TAN'-ISS
ZOAR	ZOH'-AR
ZOBAH	ZOH'-BA
ZOBEBAH	ZOH-BEH'-BA
ZOHAR	ZOH'-HAR
ZERAH	ZERR'-A
ZOHETH	ZOH'-HETH
ZOPHAH	ZOH'-FA
ZOPHAI	ZOH'-FY
ZUPH	ZOOF'
ZOPHIM	ZOH'-FIMM
ZORAH	ZOH'-RA
ZORATHITES	ZOH'-RATH-IGHTS
ZORITES	ZOH'-RIGHTS
ZUAR	ZOO'-AR
ZUPH	ZOOF'
ZOPHAI	ZOH'-FY
ZUR	ZOOR'
ZURIEL	ZOO'-RI-EL
ZURISHADDAI	ZOO'-RI-SHAD'-EYE
ZUZIM	ZOO'-ZIMM

APPENDIX

FOREIGN WORDS IN THE BIBLE

A. Explained

I. BIBLE BOOKS

BIBLE—Greek for "Books"; named after the Phoenician city BYBLOS (in Hebrew GEBAL) because from that city came the papyrus on which messages were written.

PENTATEUCH—Greek for FIVE BOOKS; used as a title for the books at the beginning of bibles, whether Jewish or Christian. Also known as Torah (Law or Instruction of Moses). The Greek title came into use when the Old Testament was translated by Greek-speaking Jews for Greek-speaking Jews, as the LXX or SEPTUAGINT (Version by the Seventy).

APOCRYPHA—A Greek word usually meaning "hidden"; used since the Septuagint to refer to those Old Testament books not originally composed in Hebrew.

ECCLESIASTICUS—Greek/Latin work, meaning "churchly" (i.e. to be read in church); used as title for one of the Wisdom Books (c. 130 B.C.) not written in Hebrew; known in the later Hebrew translation as The Words of Jesus ben Sirach.

ECCLESIASTES—Greek/Latin word meaning "Preacher"; used as title of one of the Wisdom Books which was composed in Hebrew and therefore appears in Hebrew Bibles. (Contrast Ecclesiasticus). The Hebrew title of the book (QOHELETH) is, however employed in the book itself as a proper name—that of a son of King David, reigning in Jerusalem. This is Solomon (after all his glory), with whom the author wisely identifies himself.

GENESIS—Greek/Latin title for the first book in bibles; a translation of the first word of the text (meaning "In the beginning of . . .") which served as the Hebrew title.

EXODUS—Greek/Latin title for the second book in bibles; it refers to the exodus from Egypt, the main event recorded. In Hebrew, known by its opening words which mean "These are the names. . . ."

LEVITICUS—Greek/Latin title for the third book: "The Levitical Book," since it deals with the priestly class descended from Levi. In Hebrew, entitled from the opening words: "And he called . . ."

NUMBERS—A Latin effort, corresponding to the Greek, to find a title for the fourth book; chosen because the book records two attempts at a census. The more informative title in Hebrew runs "In the Wilderness [of Sinai]."

DEUTERONOMY—Greek/Latin attempt to find a title for the fifth book, mistranslating a phrase in Deut. 17:38 as "this repetition of the Law" rather than as "a copy of this Law." The Hebrew title for what are seven Mosaic addresses is more informative: "These are the words . . ."

GOSPEL—A term derived from Anglo-Saxon, meaning "good-spell" (not "God-spell"), i.e. good tidings; like its Greek/ Latin equivalent EVANGEL. Since c. 150 A.D. applied as a title to the first four books in the New Testament. Because these books are partly in narrative form, the term has also been used loosely to mean "god-story," which underplays the role of word (a distinct from action) in the Good News of Jesus-Christ.

EPISTLE—Greek/Latin for a message or communication, oral or written, sent by a messenger (APOSTLE). In the New Testament used in the title of personal letters (like ONESIMUS) and small treatises (like ROMANS or HEBREWS).

REVELATION—Latin for the late Greek APOCALYPSE, and meaning "disclosure." Properly used in the singular (not in the plural) as the title of the final book in the New Testament; nevertheless revelation in the Bible is audio-visual rather than ideological (Acts 17:23; Jn. 1:18).

II. HEBREW and GREEK LETTERS

ALEPH-TAW and ALPHA-OMEGA — The names of the first and last letters of the Hebrew and Greek alphabets. All the names of the letters of the Hebrew (consonantal) alphabet are used to indicate the sections of Ps. 119 (an acrostic poem). "From Aleph to Taw" (like "from Dan to Beersheba") means "something as a whole." The phrase in Isa. 41:4 wholistically describing God as "the First" and "the Last" is repeated in Rev. 1:8 in terms of Alpha and Omega.

SHIBBOLETH and SIBBOLETH — Different local pronunciations in Hebrew of the same word; used in Judg. 12:6 by the Gibeonites as a password, enabling them to identify enemy Ephramites.

IOTA (JOT) and DOT (TITTLE) — (Matt. 5:18); "Not an iota, not a dot" (*Revised Standard Version*) "one jot or one tittle" (*King James Version*). Iota (pronounced EYE-OH'-TA) is the Greek name for our letter "I" or "i", representing the sound EE; when not written in capitals it happens to be the smallest letter in the Greek alphabet; used by the Greeks to transliterate the smallest but very important letter in the Hebrew alphabet, with the sound of 'y' as in YHWH. The Greek name was transliterated by Tyndal as "iott", which in the *King James Version* became 'jot'; *Revised Standard Version* writes 'iota'. "Dot" is the *Revised Standard Version* translation of a word in the Greek New Testament meaning "horn"; the Greek translates a Hebrew word meaning "thorn." It is the name of a tiny mark, or a projection, distinguishing any Hebrew letter which could be confused with another closely resembling it; somewhat in the way our "R" differs from our "B", so that we do not read BABBI for RABBI. Tyndal and the *King James Version* translated the term as "tittle" (title), from the Latin for a "superscription." [The point is not that an "iota" is tiny and a "dot" still tinier, but that no tiny clue (however unimportant in itself) to what is important, should be neglected.]

III. EXCLAMATIONS

AMEN — Pronounced AH'-MEN by most Catholics, EH'-MEN by most Protestants, AH-MEHN' by most Jews; it means "so be it."

MENE, MENE etc. — (Dan. 5:26); The menacing writing on the wall meant to the Persians (in Persian): "From Rags to Riches and Back, in Four Generations"; but to the Hebrews (in Hebrew) it meant, still more ominously: "HE has weighed; HE has found wanting; HE will draw — and quarter."

HALLELUJAH — "Praise the Lord" (i.e., JAH, YAHWEH). So interpreted from earlier "speaking with tongues" (ululation) such as still occurs. A "Hallelujah" appears at the start and finish of some Psalms. "Hallel's" in the title of Psalms means "Praises." The Great Hallel, Psalm 136, was the hymn chanted by Jesus and the disciples after the Last Supper (Matt. 26:30). ALLELUIA is simply Greek/Latin for HALLELUJAH.

SELAH — A term often occurring after a few lines of a Psalm; not an exclamation but a musical direction; probably indicating a pause in the chanting (for a flourish of music).

HOSANNA and BENEDICTUS — "Save now!" and "Blessed!" These cries appear in that order in Ps. 118:25-26 and in Jn. 12:13; they appear in the reverse order in Matt. 21:9, Mk. 11:10, and in the Liturgy. In the psalm, the one blessed in the name of the LORD (as he that cometh) was a worshipper approaching the temple.

TALITHA/CUMI — Aramaic words of Jesus: "Little girl! Arise!" (Mk. 5:41). This "talitha" not to be confused with that TABITHA (DORCAS) whom Peter summoned to arise (Acts 9).

EPHPHATHA — An Aramaic word (not a tongue-twister) meaning "Be opened!"; employed by Jesus (along with the application of saliva) in the healing of a deaf-mute (Mk. 7:34). Both the Aramaic word and the gesture were employed in Milan and in Rome as part of Baptism.

ANATHEMA MARANATHA—"Anathema" is a Greek word meaning something "set up" or "set apart" by a devotee; used to translate a Hebrew word for "set apart for service" or "devoted to destruction." "Maranatha" is really two Aramaic words meaning "Lord! Come!" When used in conjunction (1 Cor. 16:22) they could mean "Come, Lord, and excommunicate him yourself." (See RACA).

RACA—An Aramaic term of abuse: "Scoundrel!"; its users condemn themselves to GEHENNA (Matt. 5:32); less offensive, however, than "Anathema!"

ELI, ELI (ELOI, ELOI)—"My God, My God . . ." (Matt. 27:46; Mk. 15:34) Actually the opening words of Ps. 22 in Hebrew and in Aramaic; a Song of despair ending in triumph; used in part (or as a whole) by Jesus on the Cross; interpreted by some bystanders as a cry for Elijah (not for Eli).

IV. FEASTS

PASSOVER (PASCH) and UNLEAVENED BREAD—"Pasch" is a transliteration and "Passover" a translation of one of the two chief names of this Spring Festival: (PESACH); while UNLEAVENED (bread or cakes) is the translation of the other chief name MAZZOTH ("sweet," i.e., unfermented, because made without yeast.) Both names stem from the interpretation of the Feast as a commemoration of the Exodus from Egypt at which time the Hebrew first-born had been spared (passed over) by the last of the plagues; and when also the breads for the coming journey had been hastily prepared without yeast. The date of the festival, like that of Easter (three days after Passover), is calculated by the moon; the dates would coincide more often were not Easter tied to a Sabbath (Sunday). Originally, PESACH and MAZZOTH were separate Spring Festivals; the former of the firstlings of the flock, the latter of the first fruits of the field.

PENTECOST—Greek for "fiftieth"; an Old Testament to Jewish festival held on the fiftieth day after the barley-sheaf ceremony during Passover. In Hebrew, it is called "The Feast of Weeks," (Shabuoth), and originally marked the end of the corn harvest; it was transformed into a commemoration of the giving of "The LAW" (fifty days after the beginning of the Exodus). The term is so used throughout the New Testament. But since it was on a Pentecost Day that the Holy Ghost also descended on the Church, "Pentecost" because in addition the name for the Christian Festival celebrating that event. The day is also known as "Whitsun" (White Sunday) from the custom of clothing the newly baptized in white on that day. The season of Pentecost lasts either one week (till Trinity Sunday) or, more usually today, until Advent.

PURIM — (Esther 3). "Pur" and "Purim" are Hebrew words meaning "lot" and "lots." According to the religious romance of ESTHER, the Jewish people were saved from a Persian pogrom, the date of which had been settled by lots. This deliverance is celebrated in the carnival festivities called "Purim" (Lots), held just before or at the start of the New Year in March (according to some Jewish calendars).

V. PLACES

EDEN etc. — An Akkadian word meaning a "Flatland"; borrowed by the Hebrews and taken to mean "Delight"; similarly, the Greek/Latin term, a "Paradise" (used to translate "Eden") had been borrowed by the Greek historian Xenophon from the Persian for "a wooded park". "In the East" means chiefly "in the Orient" (where the sun "originates" or rises). The whole phrase may perhaps be best translated: "An Oriental Garden of Delight" (Gen. 2).

HIKKEDEL, PISHON etc. — The four Edenic Rivers of Gen. 2 probably include the Nile and the Ganges, as well as the Tigris and the Euphrates.

SHEOL, HADES — (e.g. in Ps. 139:8 and 1 Cor. 15:55). The chief names in Hebrew and Greek for the Abode of the Dead. "Sheol" is derived from a verb "to inquire";

because neeromancers sought oracles from the shades of the dead (REPHAIM) in their place of abode. This underworld realm of the Greek God Hades was connected by some Greeks (such as Socrates) with a Greek word meaning simply "The Unseen (Realm)"; Christ Himself descended to Hades.

GEHENNA – (Matt. 5:22); Greek for Ge Hinnom [Valley of the Sons of Hinnom (a person otherwise unknown)]; the hellishly smouldering rubbish-dump outside the walls of the Holy City; formerly a place where human beings had been offered as burnt sacrifices. In extrabiblical Jewish writings (such as ENOCH, which influenced the composition of the gospels) this hell-fire became a figure for a place of everlasting punishment. (Compare TARTARUS in the *Georgics* of Virgil and its use in 2 Pet. 2:4.).

RED SEA and SEA OF REEDS – The term "Red Sea" was used in the Ancient world to cover all the North-Western reaches of the Indian Ocean; so named for the red coral visibly lining the sea's bottom. The term was mistakenly adopted in the Greek translation of the Old Testament to render the YAM SUPH (SEA of REEDS or RUSHES) crossed on foot by the Hebrews in their Exodus from Egypt; probably identifiable with a marshy area of the Isthmus of Egypt, in which the pursuing chariots of Egypt got mired and swamped (Exod. 10:19).

SIN and SINAI etc. – The city called SIN in Hebrew (the classical Pelusium) at Ezek. 30:15; the Wilderness of SIN and ZIN in Exod. 16 and Num. 13; like Mount Sinai, a people called the SINIM and a tribe known as the SINITES, have none of them any connection with "sin" (whether original, actual, mortal, or venial).

GADARA, GERASA, and THE SWINE – (Matt. 8:28; Mk. 5:9). Places somewhere in a large area of Transjordan, known in Old Testament times as GILEAD and in New Testament times as the DECAPOLIS ("Ten Cities"). One of the larger cities was GERASA (now JERASH, with unspoiled ruins of the Palestine that Jesus knew); another was GADARA. But within the area was a second though smaller GERASA, built on a cliff (overlooking the Sea of Galilee) where Jewish psychotic outcasts managed to exist, while nearby some Gentiles raised pigs. Here occured the cure by Jesus of the psychotic nicknamed "Legion" after those powerful possessors, the Roman legions; his "voices" asked permission to leave him and inhabit the pigs ("the Gadarene Swine") whereupon they behaved like lemmings.

GETHSEMANE (GESAMINI) – Greek attempts to transliterate two Aramaic words meaning "oil vat"; the name designated the olive orchard (field, garden) which Jesus daily passed by on his way to or from Jerusalem and Bethany. Sometimes he and the disciples paused there, like Socrates and his friends in "the groves of Academe" (Matt. 26:36).

GABBATHA – The Hebrew name (of unknown origin) for what the Greeks called "Lithostrotos" (mosaic pavement); a raised platform from which justice was administered, as by Pilate to Jesus when he was accused of treason (Jn. 19:13).

GOLGOTHA (CALVARY) – Hebrew and Latin for "Skull-Place or Cranium." (cf. in New Hampshire, "The Old Man of the Mountain").

AREOPAGUS – "Hill of Ares"; "Mars Hill"; rising above the AGORA or marketplace of Athens. It may have given its name to the court or council before which St. Paul appeared. That court met, however, at the foot of the hill, (down in the agora) where the Arai (goddesses of revenge) had their shrine; it was this "Arai-Hill" court (named for them) before which Orestes had once stood trial and been acquitted by Athena; one of its members (Areopagite) was converted by St. Paul.

VI. PERSONAGES and TITLES

SHADDAY – A Divine Title: "The Mountain One" rather than "The Almighty" (e.g. Gen. 17:1). Often an allusion to the theophany at Mount Sinai. A title especially favored in Job (e.g. 5:17; 6:4), the scene of this theophany being laid amid the Mountains of UZ (Edom). When the term occurs as part of a personal name (like ZURISHADDAI), it is spelled with a final I instead of a Y.

SABBATH—Hebrew for the seventh day of any week; became a day of rest, and so described in the priestly account of the creation of the calendar (Gen. 1).

SATAN and DEVIL—In Hebrew a satan is an adversary (Job 1:6) and in Greek a "diabolos" (devil) is a slanderer. When personified, this power is sometimes called Belial ("Worthless One") (e.g. Judg. 19:22). In the Apocrypha and allied writings, Satan is identified with the Snake in the Garden of Eden (e.g. 2 Enoch 3:13). In the New Testament this power of darkness is twice referred to by Jesus as Beelzebul (an epithet of unknown meaning) (Matt. 10:25, 12:24). Some hold that Satan or the Devil is the sole denizen of Hell; the famous Biblical Scholar Origen remains uncanonized for further holding that even the Devil might be saved.

AM-HA-AREZ—In Hebrew literally "the people of the land"; but in the Old Testament chiefly "the responsible citizens"; in the New Testament, the crowds of "common people" ignorant of the niceties of the Law.

IMMANUEL (EMMANUEL)—Hebrew for "God (is) with us"; a name given by a prophet (the first Isaiah) to an unborn child, as a sign of victory to come (Isa. 7:14); applied as a title to Jesus (Matt. 1:23).

GOG and MAGOG—In the historical books of the Old Testament, there are persons bearing these names; in the prophecies of Ezekiel there appears a symbolic prince named Gog from the symbolic land of Magog; in Rev. 20:8, both Gog and Magog are leaders (or leading nations) of the forces of evil—pictured as finally being routed at Armageddon (the Hill of Megiddo, scene of mighty battles in the past).

SATRAP—In the Persian Empire, governor of a province (Esth. 8:9).

SADDUCEES – The "Sons of Zadok" (a priest of King Solomon's, 1 Kgs. 2:26) were a conservative party gravitating around the priesthood in Jerusalem; they confined themselves to the doctrines and practices of the Pentateuch.

PROPHET – Greek term translating the Hebrew for a forth-teller rather than a fore-teller; usually to be distinguished from a seer because he has heard rather than seen the message.

PHARISEES – Hebrew for "The Separate Ones"; a prophetic-puritanical party who clung not only to the Law but to the Prophets during the Exile from Jerusalem and the Temple; by the time of Jesus, immersed, however, in petty regulations.

CORBAN – (Mk. 7:11); An irreversible vow or oblation, according to strict Pharisaic doctrine in the time of Jesus; a notion already implied, however, as far back as the story of Jephthah's vow (Judg. 11).

RABBI – Hebrew for a teacher; a word often used of Jesus in the Gospels.

SYNAGOGUE – Greek for a "gathering"; used in the LXX to translate Hebrew words for "congregation" and "assembly"; later a "place of assembly", especially for worship and instruction as at Nazareth and Caphernaum (Lk. 4); cf. a "church" as both a congregation and a building.

SCRIBE – Latin translation of Greek and Hebrew terms for one able to write and so become a secretary (e.g. Jer. 32). Later, after the return from the Exile, scribes (whether laymen or priests) were officials who resisted Hellenization by applying (in detail) all the Law and the Prophets; in the Gospels, they form part of the Pharisaic Party.

ZEALOTS and CANANEANS – (e.g. Lk. 6:15 and Matt. 10:4); Greek and Aramaic terms for anyone jealous for God, sometimes to the point of doing armed battle for Him.

SANHEDRIN (COUNCIL) – (e.g. Acts 6:12); Greek for a "sitting together", transliterated during the Hellenistic period into Hebrew and Aramaic. In the New Testament a body of legal experts in Jerusalem and elsewhere.

EPICUREANS and STOICS – (Acts 17); Greek philosophers who stressed peace of mind and calmness. When they heard Paul mention "Anastasis" (Resurrection), they assumed that it was some new goddess ("Anastasia").

CANDACE – A title rather than a name (Acts 8:27); used for any "Reigning Queen-Mother" in the Ethopian Kingdom of Meroe.

PRAETORIUM – Latin term, borrowed by Greeks, originally headquarters of a "praetor" (General); in the New Testament, one part or another of the Governor's Residence (Mk. 15:16).

PROCURATOR – Latin for manager of a province; an office held by Pontius Pilate.

PROCONSUL – Latin for a Senator Acting-for-a-Consul; i.e. a Provincial Administrator; an office held by Gallio (Acts 18).

CHRISTIANI (CHRESTIANI) and CHRISTIANS – Greek terms with Latin endings; found interchangeably in manuscripts of the New Testament and the Fathers (e.g. Acts 11:26). "Chrestiani" (Chrestians) is preserved in the French "Chrétiens"; "Christiani" entered English as "Christians" at the Renaissance. "Chrestians" is the older term, coined in Rome by pagans who had never heard of a Messiah (a Christ) to come; they supposed the Church (many of whose members were slaves) to have deified some "Chrestos" ("Good") – a common slave-name at the period. "Christians" was a correction probably made in Antioch (Acts 11:26), meaning "Followers of Christ"; but even so appearing only twice elsewhere in the New Testament (Acts 26:28; 1 Pet. 4:16). "Cretins" is a derivative of the former (not the latter) term.

JOHN-MARK etc. – Like Saul-Paul; Simon Cephas-Peter; and Thomas-Didymus: i.e. Hebrew (or Aramaic) and Roman names of the same persons. Some of the Roman names are simply translations from Aramaic into Latin or Greek.

VII. MISCELLANEOUS

HABIRU, HEBREWS, and EBER – The Habiru, c. 1200 B.C., were an ethnically mixed and mobile group in the Near East, with whom the Hebrews may be connected. In the Bible, however, the ancestry of Abraham, their chief progenitor, is traced back to a certain Eber, son of Shem – as is that of Nahor (progenitor of the Arameans) and Lot (progenitor of the Moabites and Ammonites). The later Israelites and Edomites were similarly traced back to the grandsons of Abraham (Jacob and Esau). In Exod. 1:16, Hebrews and Israelites seem to be interchangeable terms. The language of this people or peoples is not called Hebrew, in the Bible, but "the language of Canaan" or "the language of Judah." The "Hebrew" inscription on the Cross was in Aramaic. The Epistle to the HEBREWS was not addressed to Jewish Christians but possibly so entitled because it explains Hebraic ways of thinking to a Hellenistic audience.

RAB-MAG etc. – Akkadian terms, borrowed by Hebrew, for high officials at the Babylonian Court: the Chief Magus (Jer. 39:3); the Chief Eunuch (2 Kgs. 18:17); and the Chief Cupbearer (Isa. 36:2).

EPHOD – In I Sam. 2:18, Ephod is a sacred linen garment; however, in I Sam. 23:30, it is a portable religious object (like the TERAPHIM) which could be consulted (like the equally mysterious URIM and THUMMIM).

TERAPHIM – Small idols used as household gods, as by Laban (Gen. 31).

CHERUBIM – A Hebrew loan word from Akkadian, meaning "intercessors" (Gen. 3:24; Exod. 25:18). In the ancient hymn "Te deum laudamas," as in the Apocrypha and Rabbinic speculation, cherubim (and seraphim) were understood as chief messengers (archangels) from and to God. Earlier, in the Old Testament, cherubim had been guardians of Eden and of the Divine Presence in the Temple. They never bore much resemblance to the stalwart young men, and still less to the cupids, common in Renaissance art. When constructed as objects, all over the Near East as well as in Ancient Israel, they had animal bodies, wings, and human heads. "Griffin" in English is another form of the same word.

SERAPHIM—Hebrew for "Burning Ones." Although they became (like the Cherubim) chief messengers of God, in the Bible they occur only once as such (Isa. 6). Earlier (Num. 21:6-8) they had been fiery snakes or serpents. Against them, Moses set up that bronze serpent which Hezekiah eventually removed from the Temple (2 Kgs. 18:4). In Jn. 3:14, the bronze serpent is used figuratively to describe the work of Christ. When constructed as objects in the Ancient Near East, seraphs were usually six-winged figures holding a serpent in each hand.

PHYLACTERIES—Greek from the Aramaic: "amulets"; little leather cases containing Scripture verses, sometimes worn too ostentatiously while praying (Matt. 23:5).

DENARIUS—Roman coin, the one most frequently mentioned in New Testament, made of 4 grams of silver; day's pay for a laborer (Matt. 20:2).

MAMMON—Greek from the Aramaic: "riches"; slavishness to which can be fatal; faithfulness in the use of which is commended (Ecclus. 5:8; 31:8; Matt. 6:24; Lk. 16:19).

EUROCLYDON—Greek proper name: "North-Easter" (Acts 27:14); the gale before which Paul's ship was driven.

ABBA—Intimate Aramaic form of the Hebrew AB (Father); used by Jesus to indicate his relationship to God and God's relationship to us.

AGAPE, CHARITY, LOVE—Words of Greek/Latin and Anglo-Saxon origin used to distinguish the unmerited mercy bestowed on mankind by God and by Christians on friend and enemy alike (I Jn. 4:10; 1 Cor. 13).

This totally selfless attitude is also expressible toward God (1 Cor. 2:9; 8:3).

EUCHARIST—From Greek word meaning "to give thanks," so "thanksgiving" (see e.g. 1 Cor. 14:16). A name for the Lord's Supper (as distinct from the Last Supper and from charitable feasts for the needy). So named because Bread and Wine (not wheat and grapes) are thankfully set apart from all common use, and offered to God in total recall of Christ's self-offering in Flesh and Blood; the transfigured or transformed Elements are then mutually shared.

YHWH, ADONAI, JEHOVAH. YHWH are the Hebrew consonants of the special divine name, so written because Hebrew had no vowel signs till 500 A.D. When vowel signs were added, they were those of another word (Adonai; the LORD) which the Hebrews reverently uttered in its place. Transliteration, of the consonants of the one word and the vowels of the other, gave rise to the nonword "Jehovah." Many scholars, following an etymology in Exod. 3:14, connect the name with the Hebrew verb "to be," vocalize it as YAHWEH, and translate as "He who was, and is, and is to come" or as "The Eternal."

EL, ELOHIM—A less special divine name: "The Power"; usually rendered "God"; in Arabic it becomes "Allah."

YAHWEH ELOHIM—When used in conjunction (e.g. Gen. 2) best rendered "The LORD God."

SHEKINAH—An Aramaic term well known to Jesus (and the Church in Palestine) from the Aramaic translations of Hebrew scripture made orally in Synagogues: in earlier use the "dwelling" and in later use "the shining presence" of God (cf. Jn. 1:9, 1:14 and Col. 1).

SHEMA—Hebrew for "Hear!" (Deut. 6:4). The passage contains the first great Biblical confession of faith: "There is only one YAHWEH" or "The LORD is unique". And the second is like unto it: "Jesus is LORD" (1 Cor. 12:3). Queen Victoria's favorite Prime Minister, Benjamin Disraeli (a baptized Christian) died with the former of the great confessions on his lips.

B. INDEXED